# Pakistan's
## Failed Gamble
### The Battle of Laungewala

**Night 3 December 1971:** Indo-Pak War breaks out.

**Night 4/5 December 1971:** Pakistan attacks Laungewala.

**Night 5/6 December 1971:** Pakistani withdrawal commences.

**Night 7/8 December 1971:** Pakistani Divisional Commander responsible for the Laungewala offensive—Major General B.M. Mustafa is sacked.

*"On 6 December GHQ ordered withdrawal of troops to their original defensive position. Until 6 December, the troops had not received any food or water from the rear. On 8 December Major General Abdul Hameed took over command of 18 Division."*

**Major General (Retd.) Shaukat Riza**
**'The History of Pakistan Army (1966-71)'**

*"The formation was ordered to withdraw to the original position by the new GOC (Major General Abdul Hameed Khan) who took command on December 7. Mercifully the Indians did not pressure".*

**Major General (Retd.) Fazal Muqeem Khan**
**'Pakistan's Crisis in Leadership'**

*"Gul Hassan........gave orders through the DMO for the division to withdraw to the border. The COS agreed, but sacked the GOC Mustafa and replaced him with Major General Abdul Hameed Khan."*

**Brian Cloughley**
**'A History of Pakistan Army'**

# Pakistan's
# Failed Gamble
## The Battle of Laungewala

Colonel Anil Shorey

**Manas Publications**
New Delhi - 110 002 (India)

# MANAS PUBLICATIONS
(Publishers, Distributors, Importers & Exporters)
4858, Prahlad Street,
24, Ansari Road, Darya Ganj,
New Delhi - 110 002 (INDIA)
Ph.: 23260783, 23265523 (O); 27131660(R)
Fax: 011- 23272766
E-mail: manaspublications@vsnl.com
www.manaspublications.com

© Colonel Anil Shorey
2005

ISBN 81-7049-224-6
Rs. 495

No part of this book can be reproduced, stored in a retrieval system, or transmitted in any form, by any means, including mechanical, electronic, photocopying, recording, or otherwise, without prior written permission of the publisher.

The views expressed in this book are those of the author and not necessarily of the publisher. The publisher is not responsible for the views of the author and authenticity of the data, in any way what so ever.

*Typeset at*
Manas Publications

*Printed in India at*
Nice Printing Press
and Published by Mrs. Suman Lata for
**Manas Publications**, 4858, Prahlad Street
24, Ansari Road, Daryaganj
New Delhi 110002 (INDIA)

**1:26.4 was the ratio of one Indian soldier vis a vis his adversary in the Laungewala-Front**

(two infantry battlalions or 1600 combat troops; 59 tanks with one tank equal to ten men-590, and 450 troops of logistic support units-2640 men)

To those brave soldiers of 23 Punjab who made the supreme sacrifice during the battle of Laungewala—Sepoy Charan Dass, Sepoy Bishan Dass, S.M. and Sepoy Jagjit Singh, VrC; to Major General R.F. Khambatta, PVSM, GOC 12 Infantry Division during the battle who breathed his last on 29 August 2003 at Ahmedabad; and to my dearest father—Lieutenant Colonel I.K. Shorey who died during command of 14 Punjab (Nabha Akal) in February 1963 in erstwhile NEFA. To all of them, with respect and humility, I dedicate this book.

# Foreword

It is a matter of honour for me to write the Foreword of this gripping book 'Pakistan's Failed Gamble: The Battle of Laungewala' which vividly narrates the battle of Laungewala.

Even though I was totally involved in the various battles fought in the Eastern Theatre which ultimately led to the liberation of erstwhile East Pakistan and the creation of Bangladesh, I did manage to find a little time to monitor the progress and achievements of our various units and formations operating in the Western Theatre as well. Apart from functioning as the General Officer Commanding-in-Chief Eastern Command, I was at that time also the Colonel of the Punjab Regiment, hence I was keenly following up the achievements of the various battalions of the Punjab Regiment with keen interest.

Undoubtedly the achievements of 23 Punjab during the battle of Laungewala in the Western Theatre stands out as a classic example of a well fought and well coordinated ground and air battle which have no parallel in the post- independence history of Indian army. Not only is it a true story of sheer grit and determination of a handful of army men occupying a forward post against overwhelming odds in the desert sector of India during the 1971 Indo-Pak war, but it is also a story of total trust and camaraderie existing between hardened troops, commanders at all levels and the Indian Air Force.

Having known Lieutenant Colonel M.K. Hussain, the then commanding officer 23 Punjab and his team of very fine officers to include Major (now Brigadier, retired) Kuldip Singh Chandpuri, there is no denying the fact that the battalion, particularly 'A' company under Chandpuri, stood against overwhelming odds in a thoroughly professional manner, thereby carving out a niche for itself in the annals of military warfare for posterity to remember. Chandpuri's singular contribution, no doubt, was in ensuring that his men were fully motivated to stand their ground against an overwhelming superior force, apart from bringing the Pakistani column to a grinding halt by forcing tank losses on them until higher commanders could organize a timely ground and air response that turned the tables against the enemy.

Although the battle of Laungewala has been made into a popular Bollywood film titled *Border*, the storyline of which has been partially fictionalized by the producer for purposes of mass appeal, I am grateful to Colonel Anil Shorey, who is an author and writer of repute, for having narrated the famous battle in a lucid and most readable form in this book, thereby placing various aspects related to the battle in their correct perspective. The book will definitely instill a sense of awe and pride amongst its readers, both within and outside the uniform, particularly the youth of India on whose shoulders the future of this great nation rests. They will also come to know the grit and moral fibre that Indian soldiers and airmen are made of, apart from what the Indian army and the IAF stand for during war and peace.

**Lieutenant General J. S. Aurora (Retd.)**
**Padma Bhushan, PVSM**

# Acknowledgements

The battle of Laungewala will go down in the annals of military history as a classic case of human guts and dogged determination in the face of extremely heavy odds. Having studied various campaigns fought throughout the globe in different time dimensions, nowhere have I come across any case where a handful of troops numbering approximately 100, an average company combat strength, have not only faced extremely heavy odds (1:26.4 to be precise) by way of a brigade attack supported by a regiment of tanks, but also successfully stalled the attack after incurring heavy losses on the enemy at the cost of negligible casualty to the defenders, that is just three killed and three injured. That apart, as a result of subsequent combined army-air effort the enemy sustained many more casualties in tanks and personnel thereby turning the tides against the overwhelming superior force of the attackers, resulting in their disorganized withdrawal from the battle area. Laungewala was a classic battle which has carved out a niche for itself as a unique battle of sheer guts and tenacity on the part of a handful of troops who were encouraged and motivated by a charismatic and highly motivated commander, the types of which are rare in warfare.

I consider it an honour to have been given the opportunity to narrate this unique battle. I have tried to give the readers a few glimpses of the battle through the eyes of various dramatis personae in as brief, simple and interesting a manner as possible, so that this book can be read, understood and enjoyed by people of all ages and communities within and outside the uniform.

This venture would not have been possible without the encouragement and support provided by many colleagues and well wishers. I take this opportunity to thank Lieutenant General J.S. Aurora, Padma Bhushan, PVSM, (retired) for writing the Foreword for this book; to Brigadier Kuldip Singh Chandpuri, MVC, VSM, (retired), the main hero of Laungewala for his inputs and encouragement; to Colonel Dharam Vir (retired), the famous patrol leader who first reported the mass movement of enemy forces heading for Laungewala, and for making available a plethora of documents and photographs; to Brigadier R.O. Kharbanda, Major General R.F. Khambatta, PVSM and Air Marshal M.S. Bawa, PVSM, AVSM, VSM for their documentary evidences/narrations related to the battle; to 23 Punjab; to the Ministry of Defence Historical Section; to Military Operations Directorate (MO-6) and to various colleagues in the print media for making available a plethora of data from their respective newspaper archives; to Brigadier Anil Khosla (who has had a long association with 23 Punjab) and Colonel R.K. Sawhney (retired) (a former Commanding Officer of 23 Punjab) for their encouragement and assistance, and last but not the least to Sepoy Clerk Inderjit Singh of the Rajput Regiment without whose unstinted support and total dedication this venture may not have seen the light of day.

**Colonel Anil Shorey**

# Prologue

During the first week of November 1971, in the Operations Room of Pakistan's General Headquarters (GHQ) in Islamabad, military commanders were preparing their war plan for the battle of Laungewala. Scheduled for early December 1971, they planned to have breakfast at Ramgarh, lunch at Jaisalmer and then press on towards Jodhpur. According to Major General Fazal Muqeem Khan (retired) in his book *Pakistan's Crisis in Leadership—*"....the Chief of Army Staff, somewhat peremptorily and without due process of staff study, conceived the idea of an officensive mission for the Division. What purpose was to be achieved is not clear. There was a tinge of gamble in it. General Yahha Khan called it a Unique Plan". But things worked out to be completely different.

This is a true war story of courage and fortitude of a handful of army men occupying a forward post against overwhelming odds in the desert sector of India during the 1971 Indo-Pak war. It's also a unique story of total trust and camaraderie existing between seasoned troops, able commanders and daredevil pilots of the Indian Air Force. The story unfurls in segments, through the recollections of various dramatis personae from a subaltern to a Major General, apart from officers of the Indian Air Force (IAF) who participated in the battle.

There may be some minor variations in timings, facts or figures in different narrations in this book, but this has been left the way it is deliberately, so as not to lose the essence of the battle in any way. I have also tried to include extracts taken from a couple of books written by Pakistani senior officers after retirement, amongst other authors, to substrantiate various aspects related to the battle.

The battle of Laungewala is a historical legacy, which has also been made into a popular Bollywood film titled *Border*. This film has been partially fictionalized by the producer who had basically kept in mind the interest of the larger commercial segment of its targeted audience—the general public. He has, however, succeeded in presenting the story well without losing sight of the main course of the battle or the more subtle human angle, except for the emotionally romantic scenes, song sequences and some basic inaccuracies such as the fictionalized death of Lieutenant Dharam Vir enacted by Akshay Khanna. That apart, the Pakistani tank assaults have been shown as tank to tank lined up in a linear fashion, and tanks have also been shown hurling up into the air with each hit of an Indian recoilless (RCL) gun. There are some other inaccuracies. Nowhere has Pakistan's major folly of strapping fuel barrels onto tanks been depicted, an action which rang the death knell of Pakistani tank hit by Indian ground and air weapons, which tended the affected tank to explode after igniting its entire arsenal of ammunition. There are many other inconsistencies which I am not venturing to list out for the sake of avoiding prolixity.

Nevertheless, since such battles are only fought once in a generation, an endeavour is being made in this book to capture the essence of the battle in a simplistic manner for better comprehension of curious readers who may not be aware of the conduct and technical frills of military warfare.

**Colonel Anil Shorey**

# Contents

*Foreword*   *9*

*Acknowledgements*   *11*

*Prologue*   *13*

1. Laungewala Post   49
2. The Looming of War Clouds   55
3. The Desert Sector   61
4. War Declared   69
5. A Post Attacked   73
6. Anecdotes of a Patrol Leader   87
7. Perceptions of a Commander   95
8. A General Recalls   109
9. Narrations of a Fighter Pilot   125
10. The War in other Fronts—A Resume   137

*Bibliography*   *145*

*Index*   *147*

23 Punjab troops on a mounted desert patrol using BSF camels, near the Indo-Pakistani border opposite Laungewala, a day before the Battle of Laungewala

Laungewala Post and beyond

A bogged down Pakistani tank destroyed at Laungewala by 23 Punjab RCL gunners

One of the three Pakistani tanks destroyed by Sepoy Bishan Dass by placing anti-tank mines along the route of the advancing tanks. Fragments of a blasted mine can be seen next to the damaged track of the tank

Troops of 'A' Company of 23 Punjab launching a successful counter attack against enemy troops, which had captured a portion of their post at Laungewala, which Indian troops re-captured

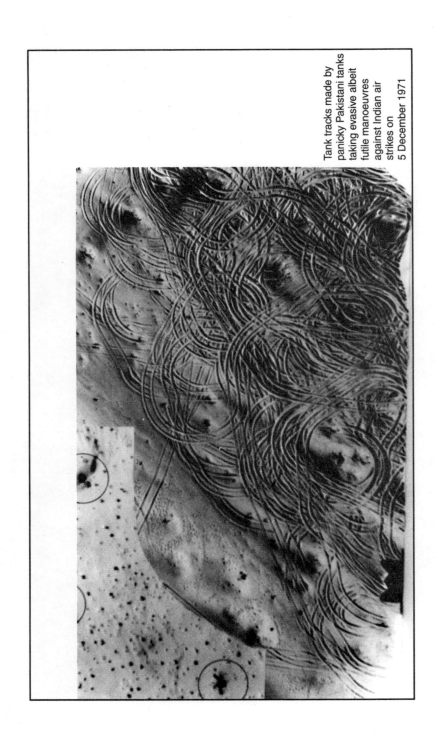

Tank tracks made by panicky Pakistani tanks taking evasive albeit futile manoeuvres against Indian air strikes on 5 December 1971

A Pakistani T-59 tank had its engine compartment totally destroyed when RCL gunners of 23 Punjab hit the fuel barrel strapped above the engine. The exploded barrel can be seen in the foreground

A totally charred Pakistani T-59 tank which exploded once its strapped-on fuel barrels caught fire as a result of Indian air strafing

Battle scarred troops of 'A' company of 23 Punjab at Laungewala after the battle

Live ammunition with Chinese markings taken out from a captured T-59 Pakistani tank at Laungewala

Brigadier RO Kharbanda (centre) poses with Major Kuldip Singh Chandpuri, Lieutenant Dharam Vir, JCOs and men of 'A' Company of 23 Punjab at Laungewala

Another knocked down Pakistani tank in its sandy grave in Laungewala

Pakistani tanks, jeeps and lorries lying immobilised near Laungewala post after the famous battle

'Hot Pursuit and Beyond'. A forward post captured by Indian troops in Pakistani territory

Indian troops at a Pakistani village on the look out for Pakistani army stragglers while withdrawing after a total defeat

Triumphant troops of the brigade atop a turret of a captured Pakistani T-59 tank at Laungewala

Prime Minister Indira Gandhi congratulating troops of 23 Punjab at Laungewala

Defence Minister Jagjivan Ram (fourth from right) alongwith other government and service officials atop of destroyed Pakistani T-59 tank at Laungewala. Standing to his left (with jungle cap) is Major General RF Khambatta, the divisional commander

Sh. Jagjivan Ram, the then Defence Minister, congratulating troops of 'A' Company of 23 Punjab at Laungewala for their splendid performance during battle

Jubilant troops of 'A'Company of 23 Punjab do the 'Bhangra' dance atop a captured Pakistani T-59 tank at Laungewala in 1971

Lieutenant General J S Aurora, the GOC-in-C Eastern Command and Colonel of the Punjab Regiment congratulates Major Kuldip Singh Chandpuri and Lieutenant Dharam Vir after the Laungewala Battle

Lieutenant General J S Aurora witnessing the signing of the famous 'declaration of unconditional surrender' by Major General A A K Niazi, Pakistan's allied commander in East Pakistan

An oil painting of the battle of Laungewala depicting a scene of the battle being fought on the morning of 5 December, 1971. This painting is presently prominently displayed in 23 Punjab Officer's Mess

Colonel Dharam Vir (Retd), (second from left) and family with Akshay Khanna during filming of 'Border'

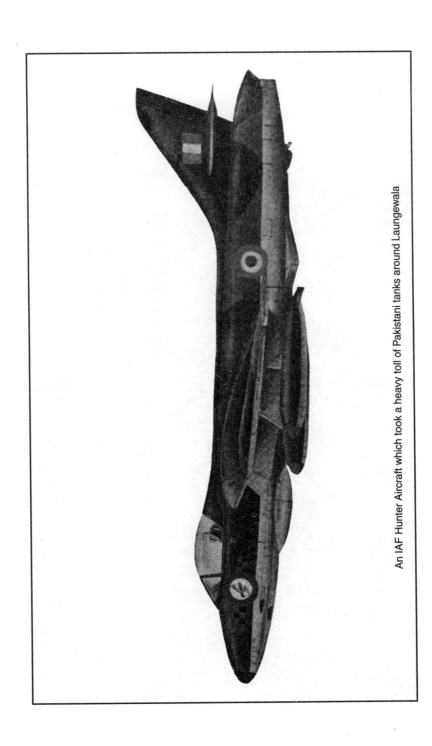

An IAF Hunter Aircraft which took a heavy toll of Pakistani tanks around Laungewala

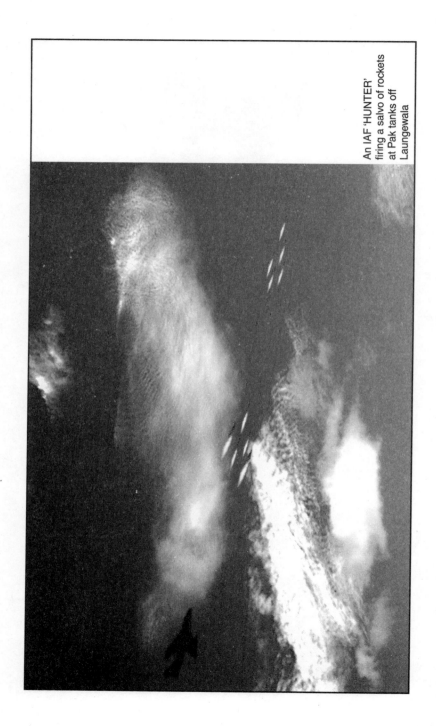

An IAF 'HUNTER' firing a salvo of rockets at Pak tanks off Laungewala

Wing Commander MS Bawa, VM, the dynamic Base Commander of Jaisalmer who minutely coordinated the air battle over Laungewala

Flight Lieutenant Ramesh Gosain, one of the IAF heroes of the battle of Laungewala

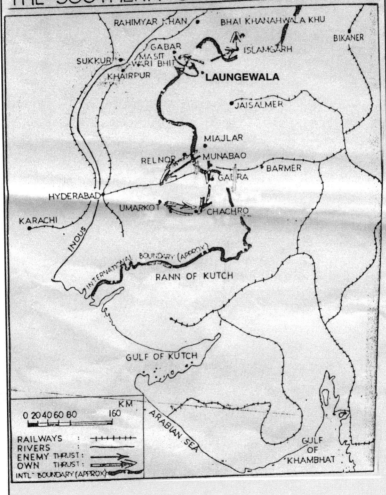

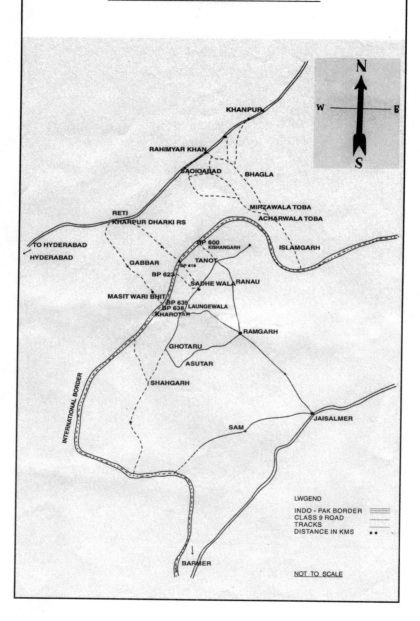

## Battle of Laungewala (Rajasthan)
## 5 December 1971

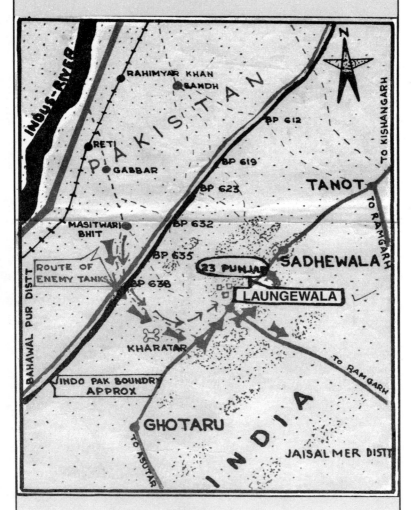

Map not to scale

Courtesy Probe Monthly Magazine March, 1980

# PAKISTAN's FAILED GAMBLE

## The Battle of Laungewala

The battle of Laungewala, fought during the 1971 Indo-Pak war, is a unique battle ever to have been fought. 'A' Company of 23 Punjab, comprising just 100 odd combatants proved to be more than a match for the Pakistani assaulting formation comprising two infantry battalions alongwith a regiment plus a squadron of armour totalling 59 tanks. So heavy were the odds in Pakistan's favour in this battle that the ratio between the attacker and the Indian defenders worked out to one Indian soldier to 26.4 Pakistani soldiers, considering the modest comparison of **one tank* to ten soldiers**; 1600 men of the two Pakistani battallions and 250 men from various support and logistic sub units.

= *One tank to ten soldiers

# 1

## Laungewala Post

As war clouds seemed to loom large over India's western horizon as a result of extremely strained relations between India and Pakistan in the wake of the latter's suppressive action in East Pakistan, a veteran battalion of the Punjab Regiment of Indian Army, i.e. 23 Punjab, was ordered to move to the border village of Sadhewala, in the Laungewala sub-sector of Rajasthan, in early October 1971. Just prior to the move, Lieutenant Colonel M.K. Hussain, the Commanding Officer (CO) briefed all officers of the battalion about the proposed deployment and tasks ahead. Thereafter the CO organized the move meticulously by making optimal use of his limited integral unit transport. The problem of transporting the balance lot of men and material was overcome by requisitioning a fleet of civil trucks through the local civil authorities, provision of which exists during mobilization, so as to augment his own fleet. As excitement spread amongst all ranks of the battalion, it became apparent that their morale had risen to greater heights.

Raised in 1966 and having just finished its first field tenure in Sikkim, 23 Punjab was orbated to 45 Infantry Brigade at Bikaner, which was part of 12 Infantry Division based at Jodhpur. It was not long after the arrival of the battalion in Rajasthan that the political storm broke over East Pakistan. The unit was quickly put through a rapid pace of desert orientation-cum-training by Brigadier R.O. Kharbanda, commander 45 Infantry Brigade.

12 Infantry Division, commanded by Major General R.F. Khambatta, had an 'offensive defence' role in the area of Ramgarh salient which juts into the Sind desert towards Rahimyar Khan in the north. 45 Infantry Brigade was tasked to provide a firm base for launching a limited offensive towards Rahimyar Khan. 23 Punjab, with its headquarters at Sadhewala, was to provide part of this firm base which covered an area close to the international border. The division, less 45 Brigade, was to launch itself, on orders from headquarters Southern Command, from the Ramgarh salient into the desert sands of Sind in Pakistan. To conform to the plans of 45 Brigade, 23 Punjab was to hold the border area of Ramgarh salient. Accordingly, its 'A' Company under Major Kuldip Singh Chandpuri, comprising two officers, two Junior Commissioned Officers (JCOs) and a hundred odd other ranks, to include attached personnel, was moved to Laungewala by mid-October 1971. Till then Laungewala was a Border Security Force (BSF) post. The composition of the men of 'A' Company was a mix of Sikh and Dogra troops at the ratio of 50:50.

## Laungewala Post

Situated in the Thar Desert, Laungewala is an uninhabited spot about 16 kilometre east of the border. It falls on a minor trade route from Sind to Ajmer through Jaisalmer. Some legends attribute the origin of its name to the trade of *laung*, or, cloves that reportedly used to pass through this place. In 1971, the place was no more than a vast wasteland comprising numerous shifting sand-dunes. Only a small water well and some old graves indicated of some habitation that had existed earlier. The post was located on a set of linked sand-dunes, about 75 feet above the general level of the ground and commanded a fairly good view all round except for the depression existing between various dunes.

The post was surrounded by similar sand-dunes in various cardinal directions around it. Adjacent to the post was a helipad. A motorable 'Class 5' road, (an army terminology depicting the bridges/culverts of a road which are capable of withstanding the movement of vehicles not exceeding five tonnes in weight at any given time), emanating from Shahgarh in the north-east, ran south westwards, parallel to the international border, through Tanot, Sadhewala, Laungewala and Ghotaru. A 'Class 9' road, capable of withstanding the movement of larger vehicles upto 9 tonnes in weight, linked Laungewala to Jaisalmer in the southeast through Ramgarh. Three kilometers towards the southwest of Laungewala lay the deserted hamlet of Kharotar. To the west of Laungewala is the portion of the international border marked by Boundary Pillars (BP) 632 to 638.

On Laungewala post there existed a small temple, the ruling deity of which was 'Mata Devi'. Legend has it that anyone who offers prayers to 'Mata Devi' and seeks the fulfilment of any particular wish, is never disappointed. The BSF personnel were full of awe and praise for the divine powers of this unique temple. On taking over the post from the BSF, a large number of troops of 'A' Company 23 Punjab made it a point to pay obeisance to this temple. However, just prior to the outbreak of the battle of Laungewala every individual of the post offered '*prasad*' to 'Mata Devi' and prayed to the goddess to give them strength to defeat the enemy and at the same time sought the deity's blessings for the safety of all the men posted at Laungewala post. Later events were to reinforce the troops' belief in the temple's unique protective powers. Apart from the temple, which was improved upon by the BSF, there were three small administrative buildings on the post. The outer perimeter of the post was demarcated by a single strand barbed wire fence, which was erected by the BSF personnel in such a manner so as to not to keep any one 'out' but to contain the six BSF camels 'in'. This fence played a vital role in the forthcoming battle.

Soon after its arrival at Laungewala, 'A' Company of 23 Punjab, under the personal directions and supervision of its dynamic company commander Chandpuri, enhanced the defensive capability of the post and built it up into a compact company defended locality with "hides" for two RCL anti-tank guns. By digging deeper, Major Chandpuri not only ensured effective overhead protection but also the construction of more effective bunkers. He also enhanced regular patrolling between BP 632 and 638, since this stretch of the border had a number of old desert tracks coming from Sind and a close and constant watch had to be kept on these. Before the post could be further strengthened by mines and wire, the Pakistanis attacked.

## Laungewala Post

Chandpuri was a veteran officer who had been recently posted to 23 Punjab from one of the oldest battalions of the regiment – 3 Punjab. Young Lieutenant Dharam Vir, then with just three years of service, was the company officer. The company strength, which is usually of 122 personnel, comprised just 104 all ranks in Laungewala, (excluding five BSF personnel under the charismatic Bhairon Singh). It was built up to its full strength just a few days prior to the outbreak of war.

Incidentally, the Punjab Regiment is historically the oldest infantry regiment of the Indian Army. In describing its seniority there can be no better example than that of what was stated by the former President of India, Dr. Zakir Hussain, who paid a glowing tribute to the Regiment during its colour presentation at Meerut in March 1969. He went on record when he said, "Your regiment has the single honour of being the oldest infantry regiment of the Indian army, and therefore the history of the Punjab Regiment is the history of the Indian Army." The oldest battalion of the Punjab Regiment, the 1$^{st}$ battalion which is now known as 1 Para (Special Forces), was raised in 1761, although 23 Punjab, which fought at Laungewala, was raised much after India's independence, on 1 October 1966.

Coming back to Laungewala, during end November 1971 two jeep mounted 106 mm RCL guns of the company had been pulled back 17 kilometers north east to the battalion headquarters at Sadhewala. This was done with a view to train additional anti-tank crew of the RCL platoon of the battalion. Strangely, a tank threat had not been considered imminent at the time, even though on 3

December Pakistan had launched a number of pre-emptive air strikes against a number of Indian air bases, including Jodhpur which was required to provide air cover to the various units, formations and installations located in the desert sector.

# 2

## The Looming of War Clouds

The chequered history of the turbulent relations between India and Pakistan ever since their independence after partition in 1947 has been truly intriguing, particularly when the two countries have so much in common. The people of these countries have a common heritage, be it historical, cultural, racial or linguistic. The similarities in geography and economics, too, would seem to dictate co-operation for mutual benefit rather than stark animosity, which is ironical to say the least.

Strangely, however, the course of history after partition has run counter to the dictates of logic and sentiment. The two states have not only been politically estranged but have pursued divergent courses in world affairs too. Having fought two major wars over the state of Jammu and Kashmir, the 1971 Indo-Pak War was fought primarily for the liberation of East Pakistan and towards the creation of an independent state—Bangladesh. Unable to bear the continuous and merciless exploitation by West Pakistan, the Awami League prepared for elections on the platform of limited autonomy for East Pakistan, and its people gave an overwhelming mandate to the programme. In 1970, after a resounding electoral victory in the first general elections ever to be held in East Pakistan, the Awami League, which had won 167 out of 313 seats in the National Assembly and 288 out of 300 seats in the East Pakistan Assembly, had looked forward to wield political power legitimately under 'Banga Bandhu', or Father of Bengal – Sheikh Mujibur Rahman.

Conversely, the prospect of a politically conscious and vibrant East Pakistan wielding political power independently was an anathema to the leaders of West Pakistan who started taking measures to deny the polity and population of East Pakistan the aspirations based on a victory through the ballot. Such a response from the West epitomized the underlying malaise prevalent against its Eastern wing. The former had been master of the two ever since independence, and wished to remain so through the continuous political and economic exploitation of the latter. In this overt power game, the leadership in West Pakistan was quite prepared to sacrifice the very Islamic bond that had created the two wings and brought them together as a cohesive nation following independence. In fact, not only did West Pakistan arbitrarily exploit its Eastern wing, but it also treated its citizens with an intellectual, racial and linguistic condescension bordering on contempt.

## The Looming of War Clouds

Soon after the elections it had seemed that General Yahya Khan would respect the will of the people of East Pakistan. He even declared that Sheikh Mujibur Rahman was a strong contender for the coveted post of Prime Minister of Pakistan. Under the pretext of sorting out political differences with the Awami League, Yahya flew to Dacca and held talks with Mujibur Rahman. But, while the talks were continuing, the military dictator fine-tuned arrangements for the large-scale massacre of the key people of East Pakistan. As soon as Yahya left Dacca on March 25, 1971, a reign of terror was unleashed in East Pakistan by the Western dominated Pakistan army. Sheikh Mujibur Rahman and many other leaders of the Awami League were arrested. Mujibur Rahman gave a clarion call for civil disobedience in the face of West's continued denial of political rights. This led to a mass upsurge which was brutally repressed by the Western controlled martial law administration. But the people of East Pakistan, instead of being cowed down by the military onslaught, declared independence. They set up a provisional government of the People's Republic of Bangladesh, organized the liberation army of 'Mukti Fauj' (which was later enlarged and merged with its army, to be called 'Mukti Bahini') and started large-scale guerrilla warfare.

The terror campaign of the military junta of West Pakistan in Bangladesh resulted in the genocide of nearly one million people and also in the exodus of about 12 million people as refugees to various neighbouring states of India, an unprecedented movement of human population in history. In Meghalaya, for instance, the refugees numbered twice the local populace and in Tripura they equalled the locals. In keeping with its age-old humanitarianism, India provided them with food, clothing and shelter on account of which India began to incur an expenditure of more than two crore rupees per day. While mobilizing a concerted national effort to provide succour to the displaced personnel, India also sought international assistance to augment its own meagre resources. It also started planning towards the early return of the refugees, but was at a dilemma to find a viable solution. For more than eight months India patiently bore the burden of these refugees and moved the international community to impress upon Pakistan to create favourable conditions for the return of the displaced people to their homeland with dignity. A solution could only be found once the national aspirations of the people of East Pakistan were fulfilled. The world community, however, could not influence Pakistan to take a reasonable course.

Pakistan's ruling coterie under Yahya Khan further aggravated the problem by its obstinacy, savage repression and continuance of genocide in East Pakistan, in spite of global protests. In order to divert the attention of the world from the goings on in East Pakistan, it declared an unwarranted war on India on 3 December 1971. With no option but to take the bull by its horns, India planned to liberate East Pakistan through a rapid campaign while simultaneously resorting to a holding action militarily along its borders with West Pakistan. Towards this end, the Eastern Theatre was placed under the overall command of an experienced general officer - Lieutenant General J.S. Aurora.

## The Looming of War Clouds

In close coordination with the Military Operations Directorate, and with the limitless encouragement of a dynamic and popular army chief - General SHF J. Manekshaw, Aurora had to plan and conduct this operation by moving Indian formations through eight states/union territories. He also had to hold together an unwieldy Bangla leadership spectrum which ranged from the disparate politicos, through the exuberant and reckless Mukti Bahini to the Bangla military hierarchy led by the proud but patriotic Brigadier Osmani. General Aurora's three Corps Commanders were Lieutenant Generals M.L. Thapan, who commanded 33 Corps responsible for the northwest sector, T.N. Raina, MVC who commanded 2 Corps responsible for the southwest sector and Sagat Singh who commanded 4 Corps responsible for the eastern sector. They all were war veterans with highly individualistic convictions. That Aurora managed to successfully mould a wide spectrum of diverse individuals into a composite whole and then to swing about an operational victory of stunning proportions was indeed his greatest triumph. It was also a triumph which could not have taken place without an intricate, synchromeshed team effort of various personalities from the charismatic Prime Minister Indira Gandhi down to the simple soldier.

# 3

# The Desert Sector

The task of the Pakistani army in the Western Theatre was to seize the initiative at the start of hostilities and to capture as much Indian territory as possible. This would have brought about intolerable pressure on the Indian Government to negotiate in terms favourable to Pakistan. However, according to Major General Fazal Muqeem Khan (retired) in his book—"The task given to this (18) Division was too ambitious.....The Division was not prepared to fight in the desert nor was it equipped for doing so....." Nevertheless, a Pakistani offensive had already been anticipated by Indian planners and contingency plans were worked out accordingly. India's western border with Pakistan is a long one and traverses varied tracts of terrain such as mountains, fertile plains, desert and marshlands. Western and Southern Command Headquarters based at Simla and Pune respectively controlled this border, with the latter conducting operations during war from an advance headquarters at Jodhpur.

The policy of the Indian Army on the western front, as briefly stated, was basically defensive in nature, restricted to only limited offensive actions. Southern Command under the command of Lieutenant General G.G. Bewoor, was responsible for the defence of Gujarat and, excluding Ganganagar, entire Rajasthan. The open and featureless terrain as existing in Rajasthan offered excellent opportunities to opposing armies to employ their respective mechanized forces optimally. In the military context the desert is universally known as a "tactician's paradise but a logisticians nightmare" because, while the terrain facilitates tactically swift armour manoeuvres, administrative problems multiply which require foresight and meticulous planning.

In Rajasthan the international boundary runs through a desert tract separating the Indian districts of Bikaner and Jaisalmer with the Pakistani districts of Bahawalpur, Rahimyar Khan, Khanpur and Mirpur Khas. The whole region is a vast expanse of sand-dunes with occasional rocky outcrops which jut out to break the monotony of the drab sandy wasteland stretching for miles. The shifting sand-dunes are of various shapes and sizes and generally run northeast to southwest, parallel to the prevailing winds. The climate is characterized by extremes in temperature and low seasonal rainfall. While winter is cold, with temperature at places falling close to freezing point, during summers the heat is intense and scorching. The hot period commences around middle of March and prevails till July. Dust-storms are common and bring down the temperature. Water is extremely scarce, confined to the occasional showers during monsoons, or to the various isolated water holes.

## The Desert Sector

Militarily, it will emerge, any plan evolved for desert operation will invariably be centred around the possession or security of water sources, the larger ones having developed over a period of time into important communication centres having tactical or strategic significance, hence their enhanced military value.

On the Pakistani side the force opposing Indian troops of 12 Infantry Division was that of Pakistan's 18 Infantry Division. Unlike the Pakistani division, it had no reconnaissance and support (Recce and Sp) battalion, which is an essential component of its army since it provides additional resources to its brigades and divisions by way of battalion support and anti-tank weapons. Furthermore, its integral armoured regiment—38 cavalry – had only vintage Sherman tanks which weighed 32 tonnes and comprised 76 mm guns, and were considered much inferior to its T-59 tanks of Chinese origin which weighed 36 tonnes and had higher caliber (100 mm) guns.

Indian commanders had appreciated that Pakistani forces in this sector would generally remain on the defensive and their tactical contingencies would be aimed at protecting the rail-road communication centres in Rahimyar Khan, Sadiquabad and Naya Chor. Therefore it was assumed that Pakistan would deploy substantial forces around these centres, keeping adequate reserves at strategic places. Actually Pakistan was capable of employing two infantry brigades supported by armour against either the Jaisalmer or Barmer Sector at any one time. However, its capacity for maintaining such a force for long was very limited owing to the distance from its bases and logistic installation. Its known disposition at Sadiquabad opposite Jaisalmer was 206 Infantry Brigade Group comprising 1 Punjab, 20 Frontier Force (FF) and one or two Mujahid battalions; 30 Wing Deserts Rangers and a weak squadron of 38 Cavalry regiment comprising Sherman tanks. Its forward positions were manned by Ranger platoons at places, while at other important places it had positioned company strength of regulars. It was also confirmed that 22 Cavalry, which was not an integral part of 18 Infantry Division but had jointed it ex 1 Armoured Division, was part of its 1 Corps. It had T-59 tanks, although the impression given to Indian commanders was that it was equipped with Shermans. Pakistan's 1 Corps, which was a strike corps, had its 1 Armoured Division and 31 Infantry Brigade located near Bahawalpur from where a reaction of one combat group comprising an armoured regiment clubbed with mechanized motorized elements could be expected within 48 hours.

On the other hand, India's 12 Infantry Division comprised three Infantry brigades; i.e. 30, 45 and 322 Infantry Brigades, three field regiments and one light regiment of artillery, one regiment of AMX light tanks, normal compliment of engineers, signals and services and 14 BSF Battalion.

Before describing the various tasks and contingencies related to 12 Infantry Division operations, it will be pertinent to comprehend the Southern Command deployment and its broad operational plans in Gujarat and Rajasthan, less Sri Ganganagar.

## The Desert Sector

This command was responsible for operations in the desert during the 14 days war with Pakistan in December 1971. The area was divided into four distinct sectors. The first was the 'Kilo' Sector with its headquarters at Bikaner. The second was 12 Infantry Divisional Sector already mentioned earlier, responsible for Jaisalmer area. 11 Infantry Divisional Sector was responsible for the Barmer area while the Kutch Sector was responsible for the entire Kutch area. Besides 11 and 12 Infantry Divisions, Southern Command had the elite battalion of 10 Para Commandos, 27 Madras and squadron of 70 Armoured Regiment (Missiles) which was to provide anti-tank cover to the Infantry divisions. In addition, 20 Lancer was allotted to 12 Infantry Division. It was equipped with AMX tanks which had lesser calibre (75 mm) guns, were light in weight (15 tonnes) and mechanically in poor condition. The Regiment was earmarked to be converted to Vijayanta tanks, which, unfortunately, got delayed.

The tasks allotted by Army Headquarters to headquarters Southern Command was to defend Gujarat and Rajasthan, excluding Ganganagar district, against Pakistan regulars and irregular forces. 11 Infantry Division was to initially impose severe attrition on Pakistani forces deployed in the Barmer sector, and to capture Khokhrapar and Gadra City on orders. Subsequently it was to develop operations towards Naya Chor and Hyderabad also on orders. In the Jaisalmer Sector 12 Infantry Division was to interdict Pakistani rail and road communications in general area Khanpur-Rahimyar Khan; to destroy on orders Pakistani forces operating opposite its sector before they could be reinforced, and thereafter to develop operations towards Hyderabad or Bahawalpur, also on specific orders.

The initial tasks allotted to 45 Brigade were to deploy forces in area Kishangarh-Tanot-Sadhewala-Laungewala with a view to facilitate concentration of the Division, to deny approaches to the sector and to destroy any enemy that may enter the Jaisalmer Sector. It was also to undertake offensive operations on orders across the Indo-Pak border to include an advance on an axis and contact Pakistani defences in area Rahimyar Khan and destroy maximum enemy forces in the area of Rahimyar Khan-Sadiquabad before these could be reinforced.

14 BSF Battalion was made responsible to deal with any threat from across the border in the Shahgarh Bulge. Necessary transport and camels were also provided for making two companies of BSF mobile. From the defensive point of view, it was appreciated that Pakistani ingress would be maximum of a brigade group, hence 45 Infantry Brigade with 14 BSF Battalion were to be deployed at four major places. The first of these - Laungewala - would comprise one company to stop ingress from Gabbar through the gap between BP 635 and BP 638. Defence of Sadhewala was the responsibility of a battalion (23 Punjab) less a company to cover the axis from Sandh towards BP 623. Tanot would comprise a battalion to cover axis BP 623 to BP 609 and thence to Brigade Headquarters or Divisional main, both at Tanot. Kishangarh would have a battalion. The division had its rear at Ranau and its maintenance area at Jaisalmer.

Since the terrain afforded greater manoeuvreability and finding Laungewala to be occupied by just a hastily deployed company of 23 Punjab alongwith a few jawans of BSF, Pakistan decided to take an offensive initiative and exploit

## The Desert Sector

India's weak defences in this sector. It was a bold plan but one which could not be well executed due to poor information of terrain, Indian army deployment and lack of close air support. Conversely, the grit, determination and will to fight by the brave officers and men of a mere company of Indian Army and an ad hoc squadron of the Air Force were amply demonstrated. The battle of Laungewala, therefore, is unique.

# 4

## War Declared

The war broke out at 5.45 p.m. on 3 December 1971 when Pakistan resorted to a swift aerial action and bombarded a number of Indian bases, namely Amritsar, Awantipur, Ambala, Agra, Jodhpur, Pathankot, Srinagar and Uttarlai. A total of six Starfighter and ten Sabre squadrons were used in these attacks. Pakistan, apparently, used the fading twilight for ease of its own navigation and simultaneously to put the runways of Indian forward airfields and aircraft out of commission. This air attack was to be followed by bomber raids deeper into Indian territory later that night. Between the dusk of December 3 and the dawn of December 4 there were 24 aerial attacks, including three on the Indian bomber base at Agra, where its runway was damaged but quickly recommissioned within a couple of hours. Pakistan, however, failed to appreciate India's capability to retaliate. That night itself Indian Canberras struck at Murid, Mianwali, Sargodha, Changa Mouga,

Chanderi, Risalwala, Shorkot and Masrur airfields. On land, Pakistani forces mounted ferocious attacks on Indian forward positions all along the western border in the Punjab area, particularly at Sulemanke and Khem Karan, and along the cease-fire line in Jammu and Kashmir to include Chhamb and Poonch. A state of emergency was proclaimed by the President and Prime Minister of India. In a broadcast to the nation at 20 minutes past midnight on 4 December the latter called upon the people of India to unite and repel the aggression decisively. By first light on 4 December, the IAF fighter bombers also struck at Chanderi, Risalwala, Kohat, Peshawar, Mianwali, Murid, Walton and Shorkot. These attacks appear to have blunted Pakistan's capability to follow up its previous day's strikes. The oil storage depot at Keamari near Karachi port was also bombed and set on fire. This attack is known to have seriously affected Pakistan's fuel position.

On 4 December Pakistan proclaimed a state of war with India. Indian troops crossed into Bangladesh. The eastern and western fleets of the Indian Navy went into action.

In the first day's fighting, Pakistan lost 33 planes, either shot down or destroyed on the ground. These included three Mirages, two F-104 Starfighters, 19 Sabres, five B-57 bombers, three light air observation aircraft and one transport plane. Twelve Pakistani tanks were destroyed, six in the Ferozepore sector and an equal number near Chhamb. Two Pakistani gunboats were sunk and a merchant vessel captured in the Arabian Sea. IAF planes destroyed six powerboats and damaged another 20. India lost a total of 13 planes, 11 in the west and two over Bangladesh.

## War Declared 71

The U.N. Security Council met that day in an emergency session to consider the 'deteriorating situation which led to armed clashes between India and Pakistan'.

# 5

## A Post Attacked

On 4 December, as part of 23 Punjab's patrolling programme, Lieutenant Dharam Vir took out a patrol comprising 21 other ranks to Boundary Pillar (BP) 635, which was located 16 km towards the west of Laungewala. It had left Laungewala post towards evening with a small supply of water and food, and after trudging for hours in the soft sand, deployed astride BP 635. As the cold December night progressed, the bright moon which had just risen over the eastern horizon tended to cast strange shadows over the landscape. Soon Dharam Vir went around the general area of BP 635 at about 10.30 p.m., making sure that the look-out group was at its designated location while the other group rested. This done, he returned to the patrol base which was located in a small defile some 200 metres away to the east. At about 11 p.m. Havildar Mohinder Singh of the look-out group reported hearing faint tank noises at a distance. The entire patrol was now fully alert. In the absence of any credible information related to enemy concentration opposite Laungewala, the general belief was that the look-out group was imagining things. However, the noise of approaching tanks could soon be clearly heard by every member of the patrol, and all doubts were put to rest in anyone's mind. The matter was immediately reported to company headquarters, from where it was reported to higher headquarters up the chain to include the battalion, brigade and the divisional headquarters. However, no one beyond the battalion headquarters was prepared to give any credibility to this information.

Ironically, since no intelligence report had been received intimating the large build up of enemy forces opposite this Indian sector, the commanders and staff officers of higher formation headquarters felt that imagination had got the better of Dharam Vir. They insisted that 'A' company of 23 Punjab should reconfirm the patrol report forwarded by Dharam Vir, and accordingly Major Kuldip Singh Chandpuri at Laungewala came on the radio-set personally and asked Dharam Vir to reconfirm tank noises, which was once again fully confirmed by the latter.

It so happened that the latest information passed up the channel by Major Chandpuri was also discounted. By about 2 a.m., Dharam Vir could see tank columns silhouetted against the moonlit horizon. Some of the tank columns were accompanied by vehicles, all painfully ploughing their way from the direction of Pakistan, and were heading towards a defile near village Kharotar, located approximately 3 km south-west of Laungewala, from where they could easily approach the post. Dharam

## A Post Attacked

Vir's patrol kept its cool and continued to monitor with stealth the strength and type of tanks and vehicles which were now not more than two hundred meters away from them. The young officer gave up the count after 30 tanks and twice the number of assorted vehicles, which included some tractors towing some other types of vehicles. According to Major General Shaukat Riza in his book *The History of Pakistan Army (1966-71)* — "The infantry was mounted on agricultural tractors, to keep up with the armour. The tractors were wheeled, and the heavy wheels just sank in the soft sand." This is what happened subsequently, and the infantry following the tanks got bogged down. "The perversity of the terrain came as a shock to the troops," states the Pakistani author. Chandpuri kept on informing his higher-ups of these latest developments.

With no more doubts in anyone's mind up the hierarchy, the brigade headquarters contemplated reverting to Laungewala the two RCL guns, which were earlier despatched to battalion headquarters at Sadhewala for conduct of training. Meanwhile, Major Chandpuri found himself explaining the situation over the radio-set time and again to his CO at Sadhewala a the brigade commander of 45 Infantry Brigade based at Tanot, and even to the General Officer Commanding (GOC) and other staff officers of 12 Infantry Division, the tactical headquarters of which was located 8 km behind Tanot. It took tremendous patience to get organized for the imminent battle while keeping over-curious enquirers at bay over the radio-set.

By 2.30 a.m. enemy artillery guns commenced shelling Laungewala with the dual purpose of causing attrition to

Indian troops deployed at the post and to provide direction to its own advancing columns. The firing commenced while the Pakistani tank columns were still negotiating the Kharotar defile. Dharam Vir soon reported that vehicles carrying troops could also be seen following the tank columns. Chandpuri was left in no doubt as to what to expect during the next few hours. He requested his CO for reverting his two RCL guns earliest.

Major General R.F. Khambatta, who had been planning for a limited offensive into Pakistani territory, soon found himself unsettled by the unexpected enemy thrust. There were rumours of a Pakistani boast of stopping for breakfast at Ramgarh and pausing for lunch at Jaisalmer before moving towards Jodhpur and subsequently Delhi. These rumours had been disregarded. As luck would have it, the divisional offensive had been delayed by 24 hours. Had this not been so, the division would have found it hard to cope with this unexpected threat, with no reserves to block the Pakistani planned advance. The GOC now got in touch with the air base at Jaisalmer and requested the IAF to provide close air support to Laungewala post at day-break.

By 3 a.m. the two RCL guns under Havildars Baldev Singh and Sandhur Singh reached Laungewala at breakneck speed. The post could now clearly hear the noise of tanks and vehicles from the direction of Kharotar. The frightening prospect of being overrun by the enemy's overwhelming strength caused trepidation among some jawans, for whom it was to be their first baptism of fire. Sensing this, Chandpuri told his men in chaste Punjabi: "Any one who is afraid to face the enemy, is free to run

## A Post Attacked

away now, although it will be a shame to the battalion and its ancestors, who thought nothing of sacrificing their lives in the past for the honour and name of this paltan" and added "but remember, I intend to stand and fight to the last". This touched them, and soon they all reassured that they would never desert him or their colleagues in the post, and would fight and die till the last man. Chandpuri, although apprehensive, had complete faith in his men and took a silent pledge thereafter — that of not to vacate Laungewala under any circumstances and, if need be, to fight to the last man/last round. In order to uphold the morale of his men he made it a point to keep in regular contact with his various platoons, sections and detachments deployed all along the post, and constantly motivated them to put in their best at all times, thereby upholding the traditions of the battalion and the Punjab Regiment. This act of Chandpuri had made a tremendous impact on his men and they were determined to live up to the expectations of their company commander, battalion commander and the regiment. This was proved beyond doubt subsequently, after the battle was over.

At 4 a.m. enemy armour, later identified as 22 Cavalry consisting of Chinese-built T-59 tanks plus a squadron of Shermans ex 38 Cavalry, alongwith infantry mounted on tanks later identified as troops of 38 Baluch Regiment, were seen emerging from nearby dunes, ostensibly to overrun the Laungewala defences. Following close behind the armour was a long column of assorted vehicles carrying what was later identified as re-orbated combat and support troops of 51 Infantry Brigade of 18 Pakistan Infantry Division. 20 FF, which was a part of 206 Brigade earlier, now formed part of 51 Infantry Brigade. It was subsequently discovered that Pakistan had not only intended to overrun Laungewala, but had also planned a two-pronged brigade attack on Jaisalmer.

The enemy armour was closing in fast. There was no time for laying all the mines, and only a few could be laid. Major Chandpuri ordered all the remaining mines to be immediately scattered around the defended locality. This strategy had the desired effect, as it imposed caution on the on-rushing tanks. At about 4.20 a.m. the leading tanks crept forward to within effective RCL gun range, when the latter were ordered to fire. One RCL gun scored a direct hit against a T-59 tank which immediately burst into flames, while the other knocked out a jeep carrying a senior officer. The Pakistani troops spent more effort in removing his body than to pursue their objective. It was then also noticed that each tank had strapped on its back a couple of 40-gallon / 200 litres spare barrels of diesel. This was unusual, since no armoured units or formations anywhere in the world resorted to strapping fuel barrels on their tank hull, particularly during war. The reserve stock of fuel, ammunition and rations during operations always followed the advancing armoured columns in sand channelled wheeled or tracked vehicles having cross-country capability in the desert. These vehicles known as logistic echelons, always remained one bound behind, only to move up on orders or whenever required. Fuel containers strapped onto tanks always posed the risk of igniting when under enemy fire, tending the respective tank along with its first line integral ammunition to explode like a giant match box.

## A Post Attacked

Around 4.30 a.m. the enemy infantry attacked the post with vigour, shouting their battle cry '*Ya Ali*', while their tanks, artillery and medium machine guns provided close support for the attack. Inspite of innumerable odds, the attack was courageously held. The tanks then attempted to assault and started closing in. It was at this juncture that Sepoy Bishan Dass, with his detachment of pioneers, started placing anti-tank mines along the route of the assaulting tanks. He unfortunately made the supreme sacrifice in the process, but not without blowing off the tracks of three tanks. The RCL guns again opened up and knocked out two more tanks, but in the bargain Sepoy (later Naib Subedar) Mathra Dass sustained a machine gun burst from another tank and was severely wounded. One of enemy's infantry assaults, too, had been held at bay due to the sheer courage of Sepoy Jagjit Singh who continued firing his light machine gun from the open till he was killed by a tank round. The platoon under Subedar Rattan Singh took the brunt of this very assault with great fortitude. Every single soldier did his duty including the cook Sepoy Bhagi Ram who ferried ammunition to the gun positions without a break.

The loss of a few tanks seemed to have unnerved the Pakistani armoured troop commanders who preferred to stall their assault, fearing high density minefields. Furthermore, apparently due to lack of effective leadership, their infantry-tank cohesion was also not in evidence. The tanks, instead of manoeuvreing behind Laungewala and blocking the routes to Sadhewala and Ramgarh, just held back non-tactically and fully exposed, as if waiting for further orders. The brave men of Laungewala under Chandpuri's constant spurring knocked down seven more tanks with RCL guns, rocket launchers and anti-tank mines. The remaining tanks soon turned around and took cover behind sand-dunes, while some other tanks started making a detour towards the southwest in order to attack the company from the left flank and rear. During this critical manoeuvre Chandpuri ordered his MMGs and mortars to open up in a coordinated manner simultaneously, and in this process took a heavy toll of the enemy infantry. During this exchange of fire, Sepoy Charan Das of the Mortar platoon was hit by an enemy tank's MMG and made the supreme sacrifice. Surprisingly, some Pakistani troops were still seen sitting on the tanks while some others were seen running about, seeking cover. It was also observed that several tanks, while negotiating a sharp turn to get behind cover, got bogged down in loose sand. The crew bailed out and, while running for cover, were caught under LMG fire, thus suffering casualties.

Chandpuri felt that unless he was reinforced quickly his company position would be overrun by the sheer weight of enemy tanks, artillery and infantry. He sent yet another desperate request for reinforcements, this time it included immediate closer air support.

Wing Commander (later Air Marshal) M.S. Bawa was the enterprising commander of the IAF base at Jaisalmer. He responded magnificently to Khambatta's request. With just two out of four Hunter aircraft functioning, he organized an extraordinary ground crew backing with a view to send numerous sorties to Laungewala by day-break. The IAF pilots at Jaisalmer airfield were being briefed on an interdiction sortie to Nawab Shah, deep inside Pakistan

## A Post Attacked

territory, but the mission was cancelled by Bawa and the pilots were ordered to go to Laungewala instead. The first two sorties of Hunters appeared over Laungewala at 7.20 a.m. and spotted tanks all over, some on sand-dunes, some heading towards Ramgarh and some just stuck in the sand. Flying low, a sortie pilot rocketed a T-59 creeping towards the defended locality and scored a direct hit, and then he knocked out five other tanks.

Daylight air attacks brought an incredible spectacle for the troops at Laungewala. The entire area was dotted with Pakistani tanks with its infantry and vehicles aimlessly moving around in the open. It was a classic score before the unbelieving eyes of the brave defenders of Laungewala. Bawa's determined pilots made repeated rocket attacks, first against the tanks and then against other vehicles and towed guns. Panicky evasive action by enemy tanks further gave away whatever advantage of concealment the winter desert haze afforded them. Surprisingly, the Pakistan Air Force (PAF) failed to put in even a token appearance. Pertinent to say that Major (later Brigadier) Atma Singh of the Indian Air Observation Post (AOP) Squadron incurred heavy risks in assisting the IAF fighter pilots to accurately direct their shooting.

Having run out of rockets, the Hunters started firing their 30 cannons and saw a few tanks go up in flames when their rounds hit the diesel barrels strapped on the tanks. Thereafter, sortie after sortie of Hunters began arriving in pairs, knocking out several tanks. Eight enemy tanks were seen heading towards Ramgarh in single file and were easily rocketed. The IAF had the air to itself and, having immobilized all enemy armour near Laungewala, spotted a train carrying tanks, APCs, guns and other assorted vehicles approaching Khairpur in Pakistan, and blasted off the entire train with rockets and cannons.

The enemy mustered up yet another attempt to attack the post at 10.30 a.m. which was effectively thwarted by the combined effort of the IAF, the MMGs at Laungewala post and gun support provided by the field battery. The Hunters continued to take a heavy toll of enemy columns and kept up the attacks against the withdrawing enemy columns which were strung out on a linear fashion upto the border.

Meanwhile, by about 11.30 a.m., Chandpuri's post had been reinforced by Dharam Vir's patrol, and by afternoon that day reinforcements began to trickle in by way of a company of 17 Rajputana Rifles which formed part of a neighbouring formation, a troop of four AMX-13 tanks, which had been hastily collected from the Armoured Delivery Regiment located nearby, and artillery support provided by 17 Para Field Battery. The Pakistanis made another desperate bid to capture Chandpuri's position, but were repulsed with heavy casualties. The few Indian tanks put up a gallant resistance but were no match for the T-59s which managed to outmaneuvre the Indian tanks due to their better fire power and maneuverability.

By the evening of 6 December the Indian ground and air forces proudly claimed 37 enemy tanks neutralized, a feat backed up by aerial photo evidence. Air reconnaissance later that day confirmed that the Pakistani thrust to Jaisalmer was in shambles. 12 Infantry Division

## A Post Attacked

was soon in a position to readjust its defensive posture suitably and prepare for a limited offensive.

Coming back to Laungewala, one might then ask as to who actually won the battle there? In simple terms a collective endeavour led to the victory. The Indian commanders did initially underestimate the threat but thereafter got their acts together in a smooth manner. It was the hammer of the Air Force which broke up the Pakistani thrust on the anvil provided by the 'Alpha' company of 23 Punjab Regiment, a battalion which had been raised just five years before the battle, and most of its soldiers were new to combat. However, Major Chandpuri's singular contribution was in ensuring that his men stood their ground against a far superior force; in retaining command and control through the confusion; in bringing the Pakistani force to a stop by forcing tank losses on them, and in giving reliable and timely information to the higher commanders to organize a timely response. The Commanding Officer, Lieutenant Colonel M.K. Hussain, moved the anti-tank guns to Laungewala as soon as he sensed the armour threat and continually encouraged Chandpuri over the radio. If the small air component of Hunters had not contributed as they did, Major Chandpuri and his brave men could have been wiped out. So no single individual, sub unit, unit or formation can take the entire credit. It is a known fact that when a battle is won there are many claimants, as goes the saying - "Victory has many fathers but defeat is often an orphan." Nevertheless, Chandpuri stood out as a towering pillar of strength throughout the battle, an act which has been universally acclaimed and acknowledged.

Like Khem Karan during 1965, Laungewala proved to be the largest tank disaster for Pakistan during the 1971 War. It was a bold plan but executed with ineptitude and without the basic ingredient for such operations, namely, logistics and close air support. Had it not been for the meagre yet determined air effort from Jaisalmer and for the grit and steadfastness of all ranks of 'A' Company of 23 Punjab at Laungewala, the enemy's plan could have succeeded. In the event, it was the deadly aerial hammer of Wing Commander Bawa's pilots smashing away Pakistani dreams on the anvil of Major Chandpuri's men at Laungewala. The brilliant tactical victory against great odds only confirmed the troops' faith in the Mata temple of Laungewala. Men of 'A' Company still firmly recall how tank shells ricocheted off the walls of the tiny temple structure and also saved the lives of many of its men. It is also a fact that a lone, freak shell fired from an enemy tank managed to pierce the walls of the temple but left the idol unscathed. This shell, alongwith various other tell-tale signs of the battle, can be seen within the temple complex even today.

The battle at Laungewala became famous overnight and received nation-wide publicity. Major Chandpuri was conferred with the coveted Maha Vir Chakra while Subedar Rattan Singh and the gallant Sepoy Jagjit Sing.h were awarded Vir Chakras, the latter posthumously. Sepoy Mathra Das, the RCL gunner and the dare devil Sepoy Bishan Dass were awarded Sena Medals, the latter posthumously. Lieutenant Dharam Vir was Mentioned-in-Despatches for his splendid patrol action while Sepoy Cook Bagi Singh, who often left his cooking chores to lend a hand in combat, received a Commendation from the Chief of the Army

## A Post Attacked

Staff. The heroic performance of the BSF also did not go unrewarded, for Bhairon Singh of the BSF was conferred with the Sena Medal. 23 Punjab has also the proud distinction of being awarded the battle honour 'Laungewala' and theatre honour 'Sind'. All this was achieved at the cost of just three fatalities while three soldiers sustained injuries. What seemed impossible just prior to the battle turned the tables on the enemy in a most unexpected manner. Indeed, it will go down as a unique battle in the history of the Indian Army.

# 6

## Anecdotes of a Patrol Leader

Lieutenant Dharam Vir, who was the patrol commander to have reported enemy tank build-up opposite Laungewala, has a couple of anecdotes related to the time when they were shadowing enemy columns towards Laungewala post. These are narrated in his words in the succeeding paragraphs.

A very interesting incident happened when I was tasked to obtain as much information as possible on enemy armour movement and build-up, for which purpose we were to move upto a particular Border Pillar (BP) 638. Having obtained and passed back all relevant information I, along with my 21 jawans, was to fall back to Laungewala. Accordingly, before moving back, I gathered all my jawans and briefed them that enemy tanks would reach Laungewala much before us. As we trudged towards Laungewala, shadowing enemy tank columns in the starry night, we heard the sound of shelling and firing of automatics coming from the direction of Laungewala. As we climbed up a dune we could see the sky aglow. As we moved on we noticed that something was aflame at a distance. I reckoned that Laungewala was on fire. We had a sinking feeling that once we returned to Laungewala we were most likely to be butchered, since I could well appreciate Pakistan's preponderance of force in the area, and Laungewala was likely to be swarming with enemy troops. I, as an officer, had no other choice but to head post haste for Laungewala, and nudged my men to move as fast as possible. Finding their movement sluggish, I ordered the men to shed their heavy loads, except for the arms and ammunition which we were carrying, and move on. As soon as we had set course towards Laungewala, which was about 10 km from our location, the seniormost Havildar of my patrol came up to me and said, "*Sir hame Laungewala nahin jana chahie, kiyonki wahan par sab log mar chuke honge aur aap hamen bhi marwaenge*". (Sir, we should not proceed to Laungewala because everybody there would have died and you too will get us killed.) On hearing this I lost my cool and, pulling him aside, directed him in menacing tones to follow me, and, if he still hesitated I would immediately remove his strips of Havildar and place him under arrest for cowardice. The threat paid off and he followed me like a lamb.

At the crack of dawn, while we were heading for Laungewala, but were some 3-4 km away from the post, I spotted a helicopter flying extremely low along route BP 638–Laungewala and thereafter it aligned itself towards Pakistan. I immediately contacted my company

## Anecdotes of a Patrol Leader

commander Major Chandpuri and informed him about the incident. I also sought permission to shoot it down, since it was within our capability. In the meantime, all my jawans had taken up respective positions to shoot the helicopter down on orders. Major Chandpuri asked 'What sort of marking can you see on this helicopter? Chand-Tara or Tiranga?, "to which I replied "sir, I can't see any marking but it is definitely heading towards Pakistan". After some hesitation, he replied "No, do not shoot it". I was disappointed but obeyed and told my patrol party to stand down. However, I really could not understand why I was not permitted to shoot down that helicopter. Even till date I repent about it profusely, quite certain that it was an enemy helicopter, but, through a freak chance, could it be one of our own helicopters? I'll never know!

As we proceeded further and were just about a few hundred yards away from the post, we saw the post aglow and surrounded by a number of enemy tanks, which I reported to battalion headquarters at Sadhewal. However, my second-in-command, Major Ashok Deshpande was very curious and impatient to know as to what type of tanks were there. He also directed me to read their tactical number and look for other details like signs, marks, make, profile etc. To this I replied that there was an intense battle being fought. With aircraft flying in the vicinity and other tanks milling in the area, a lot of dust was being kicked up and it was extremely difficult to obtain any specific details. Since radio transmission could be picked up by anyone listening to the particular frequency, almost every commander and various staff officers from different headquarters came onto my frequency to find out as to what exactly was happening in the battlefield. I must complement my radio operator Lance Naik Raj Kumar of signal platoon who maintained steady radio communication for me throughout. Since I was being asked so many questions from various radio nets, I had to throw radio telephony protocol to the winds. I was through even to Headquarters Southern Command, the Division and quite a few Brigade Headquarters who, at times, came simultaneously on my frequency. It sounded like an Indo-Pak cricket test match commentary rather than radio telephony during an Indo-Pak war!

On arrival at Laungewala we received orders to reinforce the post. It was heartening to see our Hunter aircraft hammering enemy tanks. However, a number of times they inadvertently strafed our post. At times we had a miraculous escape. Possibly our pilots were not briefed about the forward line of own troops (FLOT). When under air threat we made use of sand-dune folds and shrubs for cover and, on seeing our aircraft, we would take lying position and stay still so as to avoid detection. The importance of FLOT cannot be over-emphasized, and, proportionately its briefing to pilots cannot be under-emphasized.

Laungewala post was occupied only by one infantry company. When a tank threat to it became imminent, Brigadier Kharbanda, our Brigade Commander, thought of sending reinforcements to further beef up the post. He accordingly ordered the move of a company of 17 Rajputana Rifles and a troop of AMX tanks to the post. However, and ironically, a troop of AMX-tanks was no match to the

## Anecdotes of a Patrol Leader

formidable T-59 tanks which the enemy had. It was like sending a mosquito to fight a bee. But perhaps the Brigade commander had no other choice at that time. The infantry company, too, reached the post, when the battle was almost over. Reinforcements to be of any military value should be so dispatched as to reach on time, and should also be compatible to be of any military value.

Major General R.F. Khambatta, our divisional commander alongwith Brigadier Kharbanda, and their principal staff officers visited the post immediately when there was a lull in the battle. They spent the night at the post with jawans and stayed in cramped MMG bunkers and detachment shelters. This stay not only displayed an exemplary sense of devotion and courage but also boosted the morale of troops at the post.

Some Pakistani Mujahids and Rangers were captured during a couple of counter-offensive operations. On interrogation they revealed that their officers possessed extremely poor leadership qualities. While conducting a search of their personal belongings we found photographs of Sheikh Mujibur Rahman. On enquiring they told us that they had no will to fight this war and that they were patiently waiting for the formation of Bangladesh, since they hailed from East Pakistan.

Since the battle of Laungewala had earned a lot of publicity and it became prominent the world over, immediately after the battle the post was visited by foreign representatives and even delegations from many foreign countries. Many entered laudable comments in the officers mess visitors' book of the battalion. Amongst the Indians VIPs to visit the post were the then Defence Minister, Mr. Jagjivan Ram accompanied by Barkatullah Khan, the then Chief Minister of Rajasthan and a host of other senior dignitaries, both civil and military. They all commended and congratulated all the jawans and officers of the Army and IAF for having achieved such a resounding success.

By the $6^{th}$ afternoon a counter-offensive by India was planned. The Army Commander, Lieutenant General G.G. Bewoor, ordered to evict the enemy earliest, to be followed by a counter-offensive. At 3.15 p.m. on the $6^{th}$ a log message was received by the GOC from the Army Commander which said "Enemy is now without water and held up in sand. You and the Air Force have destroyed his tank force and many vehicles. You have presently superiority, therefore you must not let his tanks get away. His force, including infantry must be destroyed within our borders. Air force is fully geared to support you. Good Luck". Accordingly redeployment was completed by noon on 7 December, and the Division was ordered to clear the enemy by last light 9 December.

In order to execute this task, on the evening of 8 December the commander of neighbouring 30 Infantry Brigade, Brigadier E.N. Ramadoss, gave orders to Commanding Officer 13 Kumaon, Lieutenant Colonel R.V. Jatar, to capture the area of BP 638 on the border. Accordingly, a company of 13 Kumaon led by Major Bandopadhaya advanced and contacted the enemy position. Tanks of Indian 6 (Independent) Armoured Squadron, led by Major R.D. Law (later Brigadier, now retired) also fetched up. Captain K.R. Bhakhry, of 168 Field

Regiment, was forward observation officer (FOO). He had arranged adequate fire support for the numerous attacks which were led by Majors D.S. Shekhawat and Chiddi Singh and artillery support was provided by Captain K.R. Bhakhry, Major Balbir Singh and Lieutenant G.S. Bajwa. The positions around BP 638 were soon occupied by troops of 13 Kumaon. Enemy suffered heavy casualties and left behind 51 dead, including Captain Mohammed Khan Malik of their 1 Punjab battalion, (which belonged to the holding formation but was also directed to augment the attacking 51 Infantry Brigade, albeit belatedly) alongwith many wounded, apart from large quantities of arms, ammunition and equipment. On the other hand, 13 Kumaon lost one JCO and four other ranks while 35 other ranks were wounded, including Major D.S. Shekhawat. After ousting the enemy, 13 Kumaon was tactically redeployed on the nearby heights of Masitwari Bhit, which was captured by 17 Rajputana Rifles on night 9/10 December 1971. Further up north 3 Rajputana Rifles captured Bhai Khanahwala Khu, taking 24 Pakistani soldiers who were made prisoners of War. With the capture of a few other objectives in enemy territory, and simultaneous actions taken by other battalions of the division, the enemy was completely ousted from Indian territory in this sector.

# 7

## Perceptions of a Commander

The basics of the battle of Laungewala having already been narrated, it will be interesting to know the views of the higher command pertaining to the battle. Brigadier R.O. Kharbanda, who was commander 45 Infantry Brigade under which the battle was fought, has made a few pertinent observations about the battles. Relevant extracts are reproduced in his words in this chapter.

In December 1971, 12 Infantry Division was located in the Jaisalmer Bulge for its defence. Subsequent plans allocated two brigades to attack objectives in Pakistan, while the third brigade was to remain in a defensive role.

My brigade was nominated to defend the Jaisalmer Bulge. I had a frontage of little over 600 km to defend. A rather large task for only one brigade. However, the nature of terrain dictated my dispositions. In the desert, a large attacking force must progress from water point to water point. I had four water points in my area of responsibility at Kishangarh, Tanot, Sadhewala and Laungewala. Each one had routes leading onto them from across the border and all had been used by the Pakistanis in 1965. I covered all four with a larger strength, putting only one company at Laungewala. This was considered the least likely approach as recces had shown the 'going' to be very difficult for anything but a foot column.

The war started on 3 December 1971 and the divisional plan swung into action. Two brigades started concentrating on our eastern flank prior to going into the attack. I had to launch three limited attacks to divert the enemy from the main thrust. By last light my three forces were on their way. All I was left with was two companies, one each at Laungewala and Sadhewala and these could not be lifted. I had no reserves. However, I was not unduly perturbed as my advancing columns covered the Sadhewala, Tanot and Kishangarh axes and Laungewala, as already stated, was the least likely route of ingress.

How right I was. Shortly after waking up and while sipping a cup of tea, Major Kuldip Singh Chandpuri, the Officer Commanding 'A' company of 23 Punjab at Laungewala post rang up to say that Lieutenant Dharam Vir, whom he had sent to the border in command of a platoon patrol, reported the noise of a large number of tanks approaching the border. While thanking Kuldip for the information I asked him to check the veracity of the report. Our border recces had shown the going to be very difficult. A subsequent interrogation revealed that an expert guide who knew the area well and who had migrated to Pakistan in 1965, sat on the leading tank and guided the

## Perceptions of a Commander 97

column in. Lieutenant Dharam Vir was a fine young officer but I had to be sure. A large tank column on this approach would mean a complete change of the divisional plan. In fact, the two attacking brigades would have to be halted, turned round and brought back. I informed my division Headquarters and said that I would personally speak to the General if the report was confirmed.

About half an hour later Kuldip rang up and confirmed the previous report. Although it was night, there was a degree of visibility due to a full moon. Dharm Vir had actually seen a large number of tanks with infantry on them. He estimated the tanks to be at least a regiment worth (45), backed by infantry. There were also a large number of vehicles, presumably administrative and load carriers. They had crossed the border and were heading towards the general direction of Laungewala. I asked Kuldip if he could hear the noise of the tanks and he replied "not yet", so, I directed him that as soon as he could hear the tanks and could judge in which direction they were headed he was to inform me. Noise carries far in the desert and the progress of vehicles and tanks on an unknown route at night would be slow. This would give me ample reaction time. Straight away I rang up the GOC and briefed him, and said that I would report further when I was confirmed as to where the enemy was heading. A little later I reported that the column was headed for Laungewala. My GOC, General Khambatta, was a very competent professional officer. He said, "It's all a question of time. Tell Kuldip that a relieving force is on its way and I will give him air support at first light. However, it is imperative he holds on till then," meaning approximately 7 a.m.

At about 2.30 a.m. Kuldip rang me up and said he could hear the tanks. They were still far but he had no doubts it was a large force and they appeared to be headed in his direction. He also stated that he had no anti-tank guns in location. Kuldip was a steady and sound officer. Professionally very competent, he did not flap and I had no doubts about his reports. I soon realized that I had to react. The question was react with what?

A little after 2.30 a.m. on 5 December the Pakistanis started shelling the post with medium artillery. It was during such shelling the two RCL jeeps arrived at the Post. They drove straight into previously prepared positions. The gun crew had already rehearsed their tasks and carried out practice from these carefully selected gun positions earlier. As such they were well acquainted with the terrain, area and fields of fire. This forethought paid handsome dividends during the battle.

I thought the matter over, fully realizing how dangerous the situation was. I had no reserves and the remainder of the division which had been moving in another direction had to be halted and turned around. Except for three light AMX tanks no other armour was available to me. By 3.30 a.m. Kuldip confirmed not only definite presence of tanks but confirmed them to be in a large numbers. From the sound it appeared they were in the process of trying to surround his post. I told Kuldip that, come what may, he had to hold the post at all costs. He very calmly told me that he had been put on the post to hold it and hold it he would. He said the RCL guns were in position and ready, but some more reinforcements would be most welcome. I

## Perceptions of a Commander

told him about the AMX tanks and said that reinforcements would be on their way.

Shortly after 4.30 a.m. Kuldip rang up to say that an attack had come in but had been beaten back. That all was well and the boys were in good form. However, help was desperately needed as the post was surrounded. I quickly briefed him on the GOC's plan and told him to hold on at all costs. This brave officer kept me briefed during the night till an enemy tank got to within 50 yards of the post and snapped the telephone line. We then spoke over radio till the line was restored.

Whenever we spoke I reminded Kuldip about the IAF coming in at first light, and also the fact that reinforcements were on their way. I knew that the reinforcements could not reach by first light, and so did Kuldip, but he never said a word except to assure me that he would hold the post.

In the meanwhile I got news of my columns. Two were on their way back. The third could not be contacted and had carried on and by next morning it had captured its objective.

I did a quick mental appreciation of the enemy design. A regiment of tanks (45) with infantry mounted on them indicated, as per normal grouping, one armoured regiment backed up by an Infantry brigade of three battalions totalling approximately 2700 men. Heavy and accurate medium artillery fire was coming down on Laungewala post, so they had plenty of artillery backing. Against this Kuldip had 100 odd men only, (since Dharam Vir's patrol was out of the post), two MMGs and two RCL guns. Only one determined armour-cum-infantry attack was required to wipe out the post.

Using Laungewala as a firm base the enemy could then go for the division's advance administrative base about 25 km away. There was nothing to stop him en-route. The base with its water point was well back from the border and had only administrative personnel to defend it. As the division's administrative base it had a large number of vehicles. It was stocked with supplies, petrol and ammunition to sustain the division's offensive. The division, caught unbalanced, would be cut off from its supplies.

The enemy, with our vehicles, petrol and supplies in their hands, would not have to wait for his administrative tail to catch up with him. The route along a proper tarmac road to Ramgarh (the main administrative base) and upto Jaisalmer was open. What a bold and imaginative commander could do in these circumstances was anybody's guess. However, Pakistani prisoners, when interrogated, said their Brigade Commander had boasted that he would have breakfast at Laungewala, lunch at Ramgarh and dinner at Jaisalmer. Marked maps and documents which were subsequently captured showed that this was, in fact, their modified and most ambitious plan. Considering that we had no force capable of withstanding his large force en route, it was a definite possibility. What a rich prize and a chance of a life time! The Pakistani commander had the means but, I was sure, Kuldip and his boys had the will! They held the post against all odds.

## Perceptions of a Commander 101

Coming back to the battle, at about 4.30 a.m. the enemy had come in for the attack. The tanks were leading followed by wave after wave of infantry shouting their war cry of "*Ya Ali*". Artillery and MMG fire on the post increased in volume. Kuldip shouted to his men "Hold fast boys". From the nearby trench came the reply "Don't worry sahib, we promised you that we would teach them a lesson and we will". This brave soldier then gave out their own war cry "*Bole so Nihal, Sat Sri Akal*" and it was taken up by all, and soon the post resounded defiantly with their war cry. Surrounded, cut off and outnumbered they might be, but definitely they were not downhearted.

The enemy approached closer and closer but still the anti- tank guns did not open. Suddenly one, then the other fired and two tanks went up in flames. Havildar Baldev Singh and his men of the RCL anti-tank detachment were largely responsible for the fact that the enemy did not press home armoured attacks. They had limited RCL ammunition and made every round count. So skilfully did they use their weapons that enemy was led to believe that there was a major force at the post. An enemy tank that became over-enthusiastic and came too close was knocked out. The Punjabis had a good number of kills to their credit. Two members of the RCL team were decorated for their bravery with the Sena Medal—Lance Naik Mathra Dass and Sepoy Bishan Dass (posthumously).

Our medium and light machine guns and rifle fire were taking their toll. Pakistani infantry were dropping all over the place. They wavered, then halted and eventually broke.

They started pulling back. Burning tanks were left on the battle field. Enemy infantry casualties could not be accurately assessed as the Pakistani Infantry (38 Baluch Regiment consisting of Baluchis and Pathans) were very courageous and succeeded in evacuating most of their dead and wounded, even at the cost of further casualties. A rough estimate of 15 to 20 was arrived at by cross-checking. The first attack had been beaten back and the men yelled— "*Bole So Nihal, Sat Sri Akal*".

Enemy prisoners of war later said that it was believed that the single wire fence was the inner marking of a mine field. As such they expected a dense mine field in front of the post.

Just before dawn, enemy infantry trying to probe and find a weak spot got within hearing distance of the post. They started taunting our boys who returned the compliment with interest. It is said by some people, that if you want to talk about love in poetry form, use Urdu, if you want to talk business, use English, and if you want to really abuse someone, nothing can beat Punjabi. As they were all soldiers and not poets, and their job was neither love nor business but war; Punjabi was used lavishly by both sides. With 38 Baluch Regiment comprising Punjabi speaking troops, insults going back to generations were traded, with one trying to outdo the other. Having exhausted all choice abuses a Baluchi switched to matters at hand. He said "Oye Sardaro, why are you hiding in your holes like women? Come out and fight like men". One of our boys replied "You have come to visit us, why don't you come in and get us? We have been waiting for a long time, but we find all hot air and no action".

## Perceptions of a Commander

Throughout the night Kuldip kept me informed. Whenever there was a chance he went round the post encouraging his men and comforting the wounded. For the dead he could do nothing. Subedar Rattan Singh, who officiated his second in command in the absence of Lieutenant Dharam Vir, gave him full and wholehearted support. Solid as rock, he was unshakable, guiding the men through personal example. For instance he ordered the RCL guns to fire when the tanks were trying to close in towards the platoon. He also motivated his men to move from one trench to another and persuaded them to hold at all costs. He was awarded a well deserved "Vir Chakra".

At about 6.30 a.m. the sky began to light up. Soon visibility improved and objects were becoming discernible. Kuldip anxiously scanned the sky for the promised air support. He was worried that when the enemy could clearly see his post they would be able to accurately estimate as to what little they were up against. Realizing how weak was the opposition they would just roll over the post. First light was at 7 a.m. and the IAF came in at 7.15 a.m. However, the enemy was somewhat distracted when our AMX tanks kept on popping behind sand-dunes and taking pot shots. Emboldened by the success the AMX tanks were having, their troop leader bravely sallied forth in his tank, but to be promptly blown off.

The planes came in waves. Without hesitation they went for the armour. Skilful and daring pilots pressed home their attack time and again, scoring an impressive number of kills. They kept on hammering away at the enemy until they ran out of ammunition or were short of fuel, and then returned to base for replenishment. Refuelled and fully loaded with ammunition they again returned to the fray. This they kept up throughout the day till the fading light brought their gallant efforts to a halt. All pilots who took part received gallantry awards. For their task they were provided with great help by two artillery Air Observation Officers piloting light observation planes. Flying at low level they directed the IAF planes onto various targets. Both artillery officers—Major Atma Singh and Captain P.P.S. Sangha, received Vir Chakra gallantry awards. The enemy could have reduced tank losses had they jettisoned the spare barrel of fuel each tank had lashed onto its rear. For some reason they did not, and hits that would normally not have put tanks out of action, proved to be fatal. Tanks burst into flames like funeral pyres and blew up as soon as the flames got to the ammunition.

Just before first light on 5 December 71, an interesting development took place. Major Chandpuri reported that two enemy vehicles had passed through area cross-roads nearby and were going along the road towards Sadhewala. Commander 30 Infantry Brigade, who was at this time at Sadhewala, assumed that these vehicles would be carrying troops to put a stop behind Laungewala to prevent our reinforcement from reaching Laungewala. Enemy tanks by then had already been reported on a ridge known as West Ridge, a little behind Laungewala ridge: Therefore, the company commander 17 Rajputana Rifles was accordingly warned. Incidentally, these vehicles were of the Indian 6 (Indepentant) Armoured Squadron which came through the enemy who by now had reached West Ridge. They were defective vehicles and, after repairs, were proceeding to join the squadron, which had already reached Tanot.

The three AMX tanks alongwith a company of 17 Rajputana Rifles left Sadhewala at 6.15 a.m. as reinforcements, and when the tanks were approaching two km short of Laungewala, a message was dropped by an AOP pilot warning them about enemy tanks deployed in general area West Ridge. As soon as own tanks came into effective range, a rare phenomenon of two opposing tanks firing near simultaneously took place and, while an Indian tank was hit, killing both gunner and commander, the enemy tank was also hit killing its loader. Dafadar Harbir Singh was posthumously awarded Vir Chakra for this gallant action.

At 9.30 a.m. the skies were clear of aircraft. Our Air Force boys had returned to base to replenish ammunition and fuel prior to joining the fray again. During the lull, enemy artillery and MMG fire became more intense and lot of movement of his tanks was taking place. He was attacking in broad-day light with determination. This time he was pressing home the attack. One tank got within 50 yards of the post and, by an act of God, got bogged down. Try as they would the tank wouldn't move. The enemy tank crew soon abandoned the tank. As the last man was getting out one of our boys took aim and shot at him, and, when he limped a few yards away he dropped. Now unfolds one of the unexplained happenings in war. One of the tank crew crawled back, in the face of almost certain death, to rescue his injured comrade. At 50 yards in broad daylight they were sitting targets and could not be missed. However they got back safely. I like to think our boys deliberately did not fire. A tribute to a very brave man from one soldier to another. I do hope this man was suitably decorated. Later, when I discussed this action with Kuldip, he told me that at that time his thoughts were on a different plane. Had this particular tank covered the last 50 yards, the enemy would have known there were no mines. They would have just driven over the position and flattened it.

In the meanwhile our IAF boys were back and resumed hitting the enemy hard. When they again returned to base for replenishment the Pakistani had pulled back and were retreating. At 3.30 p.m. the same day two sorties of enemy planes attacked our BSF post at Asutar, just 32 kilometres south of Laungewala. The post was completely destroyed but, from the overall battle point of view, it was a waste of effort as it had no direct effect on the battle. Kuldip and his boys had won the day. For his courage and outstanding leadership Major Chandpuri was given the immediate and most deserving award of 'Maha Vir Chakra' (MVC).

I would like to mention the outstanding job performed by a few others in the battlefield. For instance, Sepoy Bishan Das, on seeing enemy tanks approaching towards the post, started throwing anti-tank mines on the route of the tanks without caring for his personal safety. While doing so, he was hit in the abdomen by the enemy's machine gun fire and collapsed. Lying dead, he had a mine in his hand. For his gallant action he was posthumously awarded the Sena Medal.

## Perceptions of a Commander

Those enemy tanks that became too enthusiastic and came close were taken care of by Lance Naik (later Subedar) Mathra Dass who shot down two tanks. He was also awarded the Sena Medal. The entire post under the leadership of Major Chandpuri was so determined to fight back that even sepoy cook Bhagi Ram joined fighting and took position in the forward trench and shot dead a Pakistani who was trying to come close. He was later awarded the COAS's Commendation Card. At one stage, the enemy infantry was within 100 yards of forward defended localities when Sepoy Jagjit Singh, LMG No 1, took position in the open and engaged the energy after his bunker was destroyed by enemy fire. He continued firing on the advancing enemy and refused to pull back to a safe position saying that he had a very good field for fire. Shortly afterwards he was hit by a tank machine gun fire but continued to fire till he collapsed. He was posthumously awarded the Vir Chakra. Lieutenant Dharam Vir was Mentioned – in – Dispatches for his fine, sustained patrol action, although I feel he deserved a higher award. By 9 a.m. on 5 December the first assault of the enemy had been repulsed.

A word about the Temple. Before the first assault by the enemy, his tanks and infantry were edging forward and encircling the post. Soon a couple of tanks from the ridge started firing, and, in the space of a few minutes, all buildings except for the temple were razed to the ground. The temple remained untouched throughout the battle, except for one single solid anti-tank projectile which came through the open door and embedded itself in the wall, just a few inches from the "Murti" which remained in its niche on the adjacent wall, serene and intact.

# 8

## A General Recalls

Major General R.F. Khambatta, the GOC of 12 Infantry Division during the war, recollects a few interesting facts which are narrated in his own words in this chapter.

As in 1965, two commands shared the responsibility for India's western border. The Western Command, under Lieutenant General K.P. Candeth, was responsible for the whole area extending northward from Anupgarh, on the northern edge of Rajasthan, to the farthest limit of the cease-fire line in Jammu and Kashmir. It was also responsible for the India-China border in Ladakh. The border running through the Thar Desert in Rajasthan and along the Rann of Kutch in Gujarat was under Southern Command commanded by Lieutenant General G.G. Bewoor.

The Pakistani sector opposite India's Southern Command was under their 18 Infantry Division, which had two regiments of armour. Pakistan's GHQ reserve, consisting of 1 Armoured Division and 7 Infantry Division, was based in the Okara-Montogomery area, close to their 2 Corps.

Accounts published after the termination of hostilities spoke of a sharp division within the Pakistani high command. It was said that one group had been for an all-out offensive, while the second group favoured launching of preliminary operations by the holding formations which would fix the Indians and divert their attention so as to facilitate the subsequent launching of the main Pakistani offensive. Ultimately the views of the second group prevailed.

Pakistan had the advantage of choosing the time of its attack. The Indian high command could only plan measures to counter Pak designs as perceived from the placement of its forces, since both sides knew fairly accurately the general disposition of respective forces. The strategic Indian aim was to ultimately draw out Pakistani reserve formations in such a manner that they could not be in a position to launch a major offensive against India, and capture a value target which could be used subsequently for bargaining with Pakistan.

For operational purposes, the border under Southern Command was divided into four sectors. From north to south these were Bikaner, Jaisalmer, Barmer and Kutch. The 1971 campaign was, however, largely confined to the Jaisalmer and Barmer sectors due to the poor surface communications in the other two. The Jaisalmer sector was under 12 Infantry Division, commanded by me. Our divisional headquarters was at Tanot, about 120 km north

# A General Recalls 111

of Jaisalmer. The Barmer sector was with 11 Infantry Division under Major General R.D.R. Anand, which had its headquarters at Ranasar, about 11 km short of the border at Gadra Road. Our two sectors were about 240 km apart.

North of Tanot and parallel to the border, ran Pakistan's main railway and road system connecting Karachi, her only seaport in West Pakistan, with Lahore. Rahimyar Khan, about 65 km from the border, was an important station of this railway. The Indian plan was to cut off Karachi from Lahore by capturing Rahimyar Khan with my division. At the same time, 11 Division was to advance to the Naya Chor-Umarkot area and pose a threat to Hyderabad (Sind). Before partition, the metre-gauge railway connecting Barmer to Gadra Road and Munabao used to run right upto Hyderabad. Partition had given Gadra Road and Munabao to India but Gadra City went to Pakistan, as also the railway beyond Munabao. Pakistani authorities had removed a portion of the track near the frontier and ran their train services only up to Khokhropar, a place about six kilometres from Munabao. Southern Command planned to revive the rail-link between Munabao and Khokhropar and use the line for operational purposes.

Lieutenant General Bewoor set up his headquarters at Jodhpur and divided the combat manpower and equipment at his disposal between the two divisions. The reserves with him comprised one infantry battalion and a squadron of anti-tank guided missiles. These could hardly be expected to influence an advance on two widely separated axes.

I had under me three infantry brigades, a brigade of artillery, an armoured regiment of AMX-13 tanks, an independent armoured squadron of T-55 tanks and an engineer regiment. At the outbreak of hostilities, one of the infantry brigades, i.e. 45 Brigade held the firm base in the general area Kishengarh-Tanot-Sadhewal-Laungewala. The assault brigade was concentrated near Mokal and the follow-up brigade was held in the Sanu area.

Pakistan's 51 Infantry Brigade of its 18 Infantry Division was deployed in the Rahimyar Khan area while their border outposts were held by para-military forces. According to our intelligence, an armoured regiment equipped with Shermans was in support of this brigade but the enemy was actually able to launch a regiment comprising three squadrons of T-59 tanks and one of Shermans.

Southern Command's offensive was scheduled to start on the night of December 4. During that night the forward elements of my division captured a border post on its route of advance. Operations were also in progress for the capture of Islamgarh, another post on the axis of advance. Air reconnaissance had earlier been carried out on the evening of December 4 and no enemy activity was noticed on the Islamgarh-Rahimyar Khan route. The reconnaissance did not, however, cover the Gabbar-Laungewala axis. Apparently we expected no enemy initiative from that direction. However, due to lack of certain resources in our various sectors, my division's mission was postponed for 24 hours. The postponement, in fact, saved us a good deal of embarrassment. Had the Pakistani thrust come on December 6 or 7, when my division would have been plodding through the desert towards Rahimyar Khan, the consequences would have been much more serious.

Islamgarh was captured around 4 a.m. on December 5. Two hours earlier, a patrol from the Indian post at Laungewala, manned by 'A' company of 23 Punjab had reported the approach of an enemy armoured column. 16 kilometres inside Indian territory, this post had no anti-tank weapons and mines. The battalion commander, Lieutenant Colonel M.K. Hussain, rushed two recoilless guns to the post and informed the brigade and my divisional headquarters of the development.

I alerted the air-base at Jaisalmer and asked for a strike at first light. Meanwhile, it fell to Major Kuldip Singh Chandpuri, the company commander at Laungewala, to hold the post till the arrival of air-support and reinforcements. It was a moonlit night and his men could soon see the Pakistani T-59 tanks and infantry that accompanied them on tanks and vehicles take up positions along a ridge some 300 metres away. As Chandpuri's men opened up in retaliation with LMGs, MMGs, rocket launchers and mortars, the Pakistanis assumed that Laungewala was strongly held and decided to encircle the post instead of storming it. They kept engaging it with fire. It is possible that a strand of barbed wire that ran around the post to keep the post camels from getting out gave them the impression that it was a perimeter wire around a minefield.

The air-strike came promptly after first light. Jaisalmer had only a few Hunters in serviceable condition but the Air Force put them to good use. Sortie after sortie was flown. The tanks around Laungewala and those strung on the track leading to it, were sitting ducks. Guided by the air observation pilots in their tiny Krishaks, the Hunters disabled a number of tanks. The air action continued throughout December 5. Surprisingly, the Pakistan Air Force did not show up. By midday, 37 tanks and 138 other vehicles had been written off. It later transpired that the enemy had launched this offensive without arranging for air-support.

Documents captured from the assaulting troops revealed that the Pakistanis had planned to outflank the Indian troops deployed in the Tanot-Kishangarh area. They expected to have breakfast at Laungewala and lunch at Jaisalmer. Coming as they did without any air-cover and, as it later turned out, without enough water and food, their venture was extremely foolish. But it did mess up General Bewoor's plans.

General Manekshaw was furious when he noticed that no advantage was being taken of the enemy's discomfiture. On his urging, Bewoor ordered my division to go on the offensive and "destroy the enemy force quickly and, if possible, by last light December 8". Bewoor, however, stipulated that the divisional plan should be based on brigade attacks and that I should submit my plan for his approval by 11 a.m. the next day, that is December 7.

This dithering apparently angered Manekshaw. He felt that there was no question of set-piece attacks as visualized by the Army Commander; and all that was required was a bold pursuit before the enemy recovered its breath and got away. As a last resort, Manekshaw sent a personal message to me on December 7 to get on with the job, which I did. However, the Pakistan high command was quick to act. It replaced Major General BM Mustafa, commander of its 18 Division who was responsible for mounting the offensive, alongwith the Brigade Commander. Major General Abdul Hameed Khan, the new divisional commander seized the initiative and promptly ordered a hasty withdrawal. My forces followed and fought a few rear-guard actions near the frontier, and thereafter about 640 square km of the Pakistani Thar Desert was captured. According to our records, out of the total Pakistani loss of 37 tanks and 138 other vehicles, we retained 24 tanks, five field guns, four Bofors and 103 vehicles in this offensive. Whatever they could retrieve they managed to take away while withdrawing. Meanwhile the Southern Command focus turned towards the operation in the Kutch Sector.

Opposite 11 Division, too, the enemy had just one brigade group, with para-military personnel holding frontier posts. Major General Anand deployed one infantry brigade group in his firm base in the Gadra Road-Munabao area, near the frontier; while the rest of his division was held in the rear. To assist him, 10 Para Commando (less a group) was to operate in a ground role against enemy lines of communication. The success of the division depended largely on the speed with which the rail-track between Munabao and Khokhropar could be made operational. The advance began on the evening of December 4. By December 5 the leading brigade took Khokhropar against light opposition and, the brigade holding the firm base took Gadra City and Khinsar.

The road beyond Khokhropar was found to be a mere desert track. Our intelligence had reported it earlier as a tarmac highway. This meant the laying of a duck-board road for which resources were woefully inadequate. By December 7 the engineers were able to run the first train to Khokhropar but it was strafed from the air soon after its arrival there. The para commandos crossed into Pakistan after dusk on December 5. Their raid on Chachro took place in the early hours of December 7. They cleared the town, capturing nearly a score of prisoners and a good quantity of arms and ammunition. On the following night they operated against Virawah and later against Nagar Parkar, after which they returned to their base.

By the evening of December 8, the leading brigade had arrived in front of a high feature called Parbat Ali. That day the Pakistanis attacked the leading Indian elements, but were thrown back. By December 11 the follow-up brigade was also leaning on Parbat Ali. The first major engagement in this sector took place in the early hours of December 13, when the leading brigade put in a silent attack and captured Parbat Ali after a stiff battle. The enemy left behind 57 dead and 35 prisoners. It later put in three counter-attacks to retake the position, failing each time. Meanwhile, efforts continued to push forward the duckboard road and to build up for the attack on Naya Chor.

However, the cease-fire was declared while 11 Division was still building up for its projected attack on Naya Chor. The BSF had done well in the Bikaner and Kutch Sectors, capturing about 50 enemy border posts which had either been vacated by the Rangers or Mujahids, or where opposition was light. The Rajasthan campaign ended before Southern Command could reach the green belt in Sindh. The extent of territory it captured was quite large–12, 200 square km.

Major General Fazal Muqeem in his book *Pakistan's Crisis in Leadership* states that 18 Infantry Division was responsible for a 560 mile front from Rahimyar Khan to the Rann of Kutch, and was tasked to defend the area east of Indus River. The overall plan was purely defensive. However, at a later stage their COAS, while on a visit to the formation somewhat peremptorily and without due staff study concurred the idea of an offensive plan for this division inspite of its paucity of resources. What purpose was to be achieved by the offensive is not clear. However, the plan produced by the general staff as a whole was a viable one and had a tinge of gamble in it. It suited the Pakistan character, and was dubbed as a "unique plan" by General Yahya Khan who felt that its success was certain, if launched in time.

According to plans the offensive was to be launched on night 3 December with two brigades along the Laungewala approach, but was delayed by 24 hours due to 'logistic problems.' The task given to 18 Infantry Division was too ambitious, the division was neither prepared to fight in the desert nor was it equipped for doing so. Its troops were not conditioned for moving in the desert and the logistic build up was not sufficient to support the operation. Major General B.M. Mustafa, the General Officer Commanding (GOC) of 18 Infantry Division, claims that he had made this amply clear and accepted the task only on the condition that vehicles fitted with sand tyres and possessing cross-country mobility be provided to him. The only unit which was fit for and capable of moving on sand was one T-59 tank regiment, and without air support the operations of 18 Infantry Division were foredoomed under the circumstances. Their advance, therefore, was bound to end in confusion.

Immediately after the attack had been launched, all communication with the Divisional Headquarters broke off and the progress could not be ascertained till 10.30 a.m. on 5 December. Chaos also prevailed due to the fact that one column, which was supposed to arrive at Laungewala, did not reach there on time, but arrived much later. Also a large number of vehicles, guns and tanks had got bogged down in sand. The Indian Air Force proved to be master of the skies. It was very active during the day and succeeded in destroying 25 tanks and a number of other vehicles and equipment at leisure. The attacking force was beset with an acute shortage of ammunition, fuel and water. The GOC, 18 Infantry Division foresaw a disaster if supplies were not air dropped.

By 6 December, it was clear that the PAF based at Hasroor near Karachi could not provide close support. Major General Abdul Hameed Khan who took over the Division from Major General Mustafa on 6 December, ordered it to withdraw to its original position. Mercifully for the Pakistanis, we did not pursue this withdrawal relentlessly.

This was the first time that the Indian Army undertook fairly large-scale operations in the desert. From the course of events it would appear that the planners of the campaign

# A General Recalls 119

did not pay adequate attention to the problems of movement and maintenance in the terrain in which the troops were to operate. They were apparently guided by the experience of campaigns in the western desert of North Africa, where many Indian divisions fought the Axis forces during World War II.

The Thar Desert, however, is quite different from the African one. The latter allows free movement of wheeled traffic over many interior areas and most of the coastal region, and Allied armies could move cross-country on wide fronts. On the other hand, the soft sand of Thar Desert does not generally permit movement of wheeled traffic off the road. Though 'balloon' or sand channeled tyres were issued to our formations, these soon wore off and replacements were not forthcoming. Provision had been made for laying duckboard tracks, but the material available to the two divisions was found to be woefully insufficient for various tasks. Water was another big problem. Although plastic containers and Braithwaite tanks were given to units, but the carriage of water to forward areas became difficult due to the shortage of water bowsers. Besides the inadequacy of engineer resources, a big handicap was the lack of accurate intelligence, particularly regarding the state of communications across the border.

A comparison of the performance of the Indian Army on the eastern and western fronts is inevitable. While the achievement in the east was impressive by any standards, there were mixed results in the west. With one or two exceptions, even the limited offensives which were attempted in the west either did not get off the ground, or crawled laboriously till the cease-fire brought them to a halt. In this comparison, however, one should not lose sight of a basic difference between the two fronts. In East Pakistan, the Indian Army fought a single campaign that had only one objective. All efforts and resources were used for its attainment. In the west, it was not a single campaign, but a series of operations, which were essentially defensive in character. Their aim was to tie down enemy reserves, so that it should not be in a position to mount a major offensive. In the event, this aim was realized, though the reasons for Pakistan not launching such an offensive could be political and not entirely related to the military situation.

On December 16, after the surrender of his army in East Pakistan, President Yahya Khan made a broadcast to his people that it was merely the loss of a battle and that the war would go on. The Indian government, however, had no intention of prolonging the conflict as that would mean further loss of life and property and suffering for countless people. Accordingly, Prime Minister Indira Gandhi announced in Parliament on December 17 that Indian armed forces had been given instructions to cease operations from 8 p.m. that day on all fronts in the west.

It was for the first time in the history of Indo-Pak conflicts that a decision to end hostilities was not dictated by the UN or an external mediator. President Yahya Khan kept his people in suspense for several hours after the Indian announcement. However, the realities of the situation must have dawned upon him soon enough, for he accepted the cease-fire before the dead line fixed by

# A General Recalls 121

India. It is unlikely that he was not aware about the reinforcement of the Western Theatre by India, with troops withdrawn from the East. A part of II Corps had begun moving to Punjab, and the first troops had arrived there on December 13.

Some people later asserted that India wanted to destroy West Pakistan after finishing the campaign in the east and that the cease-fire was announced under pressure from a particular country or countries. I happened to ask Field Marshal Manekshaw whether there was any truth in this assertion. "There was no pressure on me or the Prime Minister", he said. "And I can't believe that any country can put pressure on Indira Gandhi", he said with his typical smile.

In terms of time we had been preparing for this offensive in Southern Command for much longer than the Pakistanis, who started only in November. Our preparations were deliberate. The Pakistanis, on the other hand, were fighting with their backs to the wall, having lost out in the East. Their 18 Infantry Division was overstreched and had practically no offensive capability. Yet, they launched an offensive in the Jaisalmer Sector that forced us to go on the defensive and shelve our offensive plans temporarily. There is no doubt that the Pakistanis threw a spanner in our wheels. Our intention to hit their main communication artery was thwarted by their unexpected ingress near Laungewala.

I now feel that the Pakistani offensive was essentially a gamble; an attempt to halt our offensive in both 11 and 12 Infantry Divisional sectors. Either of our thrusts would have seriously threatened its vital rail road communication, that run along the Indus River. To this, it has always been very sensitive. Therefore, it tried to stop us with whatever forces it could spare. The fact that we did not reach the Indus, despite our superiority and better planning, was his gain and this is what he had set out to achieve.

The Pakistanis, no doubt, knew through whatever sources our intended offensive in the Jaisalmer sector. Whether they knew the details is a matter of conjecture. Even then they could not capitalize on this. They launched their offensive without Air Defence (AD) cover. Moreover, their tank commanders appeared to have had very little information about the going. They got bogged down south of Laungewala on the Indian side. We failed to detect their concentration for offensive and to make provision for it in our offensive plans.

There is absolutely no doubt that the Indian Air Force deserved all the credit for giving a severe blow to the Pakistani Army. Had it not been for the Air Force, stopping even a regiment of armour in these vast deserts would have been rather difficult. I must emphasise that they responded fast, they responded effectively, and did support with imagination and flexibility. The base commander at Jaisalmer was given total freedom to execute his missions and was taken off from other commitments, planned for them earlier. I have reason to be proud of their actions.

Finally, the battles in the desert sector have been summed up most appropriately by Brian Cloughley in his book 'A History of Pakistan Army-Wars and Insurrections'. "11 and 12 (Indian) Divisions managed to take 4,765 square miles of Pakistan territory, albert all desert.....The whole sorry tale of operations may best be summed up in the words of Major General Shaukat Riza: 'In 1971, while neck deep in the quagmire of civil war, the Army was hurled against an enemy better equipped, better organised, better trained and larger in numbers. And, to crown every thing, we seemed to have no national objective except a cease-fire."

# 9

## Narrations of a Fighter Pilot

Since the Indian Air Force played a major role in the battle of Laungewala, I felt it appropriate to obtain the views of some of the prominent IAF fighter pilots who were intimately involved with the battle. Therefore the versions of Wing Comander MS Bawa, VM, and a couple of other pilots were obtained through interviews and various newspaper/journal publications, and then meshed in this chapter chronologically for enhanced effect. Incidentally Bawa (afffectionately known as 'Minhi' by his colleagues), who was the IAF Base Commander at Jaisalmer, personally conducted the air battle over Laungewala, and is in possession of a meticulously maintained War Diary till date.

Before describing the air battle it may be recalled that ominous war clouds had been skirting across the Indian sub-continent much before Pakistan's surprise pre-emptive air strike that came on 3 Dec 1971. Our defence planners had predicted that, in the event of an exigency of a third round between India and Pakistan, Rajasthan sector would become a casualty of enemy armour unless we could position ours to counterbalance it. But the enemy had a wide choice. There were four different places from where an attack was feared, and the most likely strike was assumed to be coming from Rahimyar Khan, one of the strongest Pak military bases. Laungewala was not on our cards. It was held by a company of Indian Army. As the Indian armour was being shifted to the area opposite Rahimyar Khan, Pakistanis sprang a surprise, they attacked Laungewala from Gabbar with a regiment of T-59 Chinese tanks accompanied by infantry troops of a Brigade strength.

In the history of every country there arises a moment of crisis; a moment which gravely threatens its security and sovereignty. At moments like these there come to the forefront ordinary mortals who change the course of history. Such a moment arose for India on 5 and 6 December 1971 when Pakistan launched an armoured thrust at Laungewala in the Jaisalmer district of Rajasthan. In the forefront, to baulk the aggressor, were the Indian Air Force personnel.

There are many instances quoted in the annals of modern warfare wherein air support, or lack of it, has tilted the outcome of land battle one way or the other. The battle of Laungewala stands out as one of the finest examples of air support to the army, mainly because it was a direct and dramatic confrontation between armour and aircraft. Laungewala, infact, turned out to be the Waterloo of Pakistani armour. The pilots of the Operational Training

Unit (OTU), flying Hunter aircraft, played a most decisive role in the "battle of Laungewala".

The 1965 Kutch operations revealed the void that existed in the defences in Rajasthan sector. It prompted the Government of India to order construction of airfields at Jaisalmer and Utterlai. The construction of Jaisalmer airfield commenced in 1967 and was completed in 1970. 14 Care and Maintenance Unit (CMU) was formed on 13 February 1967 and was entrusted with the task of looking after the assets that were created at Jaisalmer. The role of 14 CMU was to provide minimum basic facilities to aircraft, as and when required, to operate from the airfield.

The 14 CMU, christened 122 Squadron for operations, moved a detachment to Jaisalmer with four Hunters for close support duties and two trainers for Air Defence (AD) duties. Our 12 Infantry Division was deployed in Ramgarh-Tanot sector with an aim to capture the main road/rail communication line between Punjab and Sind, and subsequently threaten Rahimyar Khan airfield from where enemy air support was envisaged.

On Pakistani side, their 18 Infantry Division was entrusted with a very vast area of responsibility of approximately 550 miles from Rahimyar Khan to the Rann of Kutch. The overall plan given to their Division was to fight a defensive battle. However, at a later stage, its commanders decided to venture into an armour offensive with a tinge of gamble. Their force comprised a regiment of T-59 tanks, one squadron of Sherman tanks, a field and medium regiment of artillery and a 'fauj' of about 2500 men.

The balloon finally went up on the evening of 3 December 71 when the PAF launched a pre-emptive strike against a number of Indian airfields. On our side, the first two parts of the dictum – 'disperse, secure and react', were already in force. All assets on our airfields were already spread out. All aircraft and most of the vehicles were in concrete blast pens.

The leading column of tanks bypassed the border outpost (BOP) opposite Laungewala past midnight, with the probable intention of cutting off supply lines of 12 Infantry Division between Jaisalmer and Ramgarh, and possibly to capture Jaisalmer airfield, so useful to progress of operations. Subsequently, they would have had the whole hinterland available to run through. It was a masterly plan and surprise had been achieved. The patrol leader and company commander at Laungewala passed this information of suspected movement to the Division Headquarters, which was not taken seriously. The lead tanks did not engage the company position at Laungewala. Instead, this column of tanks elected to turn about a few kilometres short of Ramgarh to investigate why their rear echelons were not catching up. The increase in noise level of these tanks prompted the patrol leader and the company commander to inform the Division Headquarters once again about their apprehensions regarding movement of enemy tanks. This turning about of enemy tanks was a fatal mistake committed by them which changed the course of the war in this sector as they were 'day-lighted'. Since no anti-tank weapons were available at Jaisalmer, Minhi Bawa, the Base Commander ordered the use of guns and rockets as anti-tank weapons. Leaving behind two Hunter trainers for AD duties, the remaining four fighters were prepared for strike role.

The sun was still below the horizon, and as the first pair of Hunters flown by Squadron Leader Romesh Gosain and Flight Lieutenant Das zoomed in, they didn't have to look far for a wonderful sight : tanks and vehicles swarming all over, some of them even neatly lined up in a row on the road to Ramgarh. A few of them were on the move kicking up columns of dust in their wake. Spotting was no problem since the Pakistani T-59 was similar to Indian T-55 tanks. An Army AOP Pilot, Major Atma Singh, confirmed that these were Pakistani tanks and there was no Indian armour here. One of the Hunter pilots started counting the tanks on RT (radio-telephony) one, two, three ..... 19, 20, 21. This was monitored by the Base Commander in the Cap Combat Control (CCC) and the next mission was launched. On reaching the target area they found about 30 enemy tanks menacingly threatening the area. In a series of bold rocket attacks they destroyed six or seven of them. Making a quick calculation of the immensity of enemy's strength, they called for additional air strikes on the radio. In response, Squadron Leader R.N. Bali and Flight Lieutenant Deepak Yadav scoured miles of air space over the area destroying many more tanks.

In the next wave came Hunters flown by Squadron Leader S.F. Tully and Flight Lieutenant K.S. (Kookie) Suresh. "There was no need for target hunting. Many tanks were already ablaze and now we saw at least 30 tanks which resorted to intense ack-ack (anti aircraft) fire. It was like passing through a screen of smoke and fire. In one pass, we destroyed two tanks each and damaged at least six or seven", recalled Flight Lieutenant Suresh. While engaged in these ferocious attacks, Suresh had a narrow escape. A tank fired its main gun at him. Blinded by the flash, dust and smoke, and also probably because of the shock wave of the shell bursting close to him he initiated pull out a bit late. As his aircraft mushed, its tail end grazed a sand-dune. He, however, managed to handle the aircraft well and it continued to fly. Undettered, he made two more passes against the same tank and set it on fire. Despite the aircraft's reduced performance and slight damage to its tail section the young pilot brought it back to base where it was immediately made air worthy. Post-flight inspection revealed that the bottom portion of the tail-pipe was squashed. A portion of the exhaust was also missing, 'Kookie' later wrote in the operation diary: "I now have full faith in God and in the Hunter".

In the next sortie went Squadron Leader Jagbir Singh and Flight Lieutenant G. Kapoor. Following the blaze already trailed by previous pilots, they, too, caused havoc on enemy tanks which were thrown helter skelter. Another tank burst into flames somewhere among the dunes, and panic gripped the tank crew. They started moving the tanks in a zig-zag fashion, criss-crossing each other's tracks in a desperate bid to escape the Hunters, which had tasted blood.

Flight Lieutenant Romesh Gosain wrote in his report, "Tanks started manoeuvering to get behind sand-dunes and moved in circles to avoid direct hits, but they had no escape". He alone accounted for six tanks. His colleague too had his fair share. In a few minutes since their appearance this outlandish border post turned ghoulish with burning tanks strewn all around. They soon ran out of rockets, but their fuel tanks were almost full and front gun (FG) ammunition intact. Moreover, the battle fever had caught on. "I wanted to demoralize the enemy with FG ammunition, even though it is not very effective", said Gosain, so he circled around and made a low pass hugging the ground. He then noticed that Pak tanks were carrying fuel barrels strapped at the rear, perhaps to avoid hassles of replenishment in a fluid war situation. That proved to be a veritable death-trap. Fuel barrels with their highly inflammable content started bursting into horrendous flames once hit with bullets from close range. Trapped inside the raging inferno the tank crew died a horrible death. While a few others, in desperation, left their charge and ran for their lives.

"I was quite surprised", Gosain said later, "when a tank burst into flames after a hit from my gun". "Eureka! It works!", was his first reaction, and he pressed on with new-found zeal.

The battleground now looked like a huge graveyard of Pak tanks. Few were blazing, some were smouldering, some had bogged down in the sands, still some other lay abandoned. When the next pair of Hunters came to relieve them, Gosain and Das turned back but not before they had rendered the sands of Laungewala into a blazing inferno.

As the first pair of Hunters banked to return to the air base, already two other Hunters were positioned in the blast-pens, oiled and armed, poised for immediate take-off. A chain reaction was thus established successfully. "The moment we took-off", Gosain wrote in his diary, "the engineers got down to repair our bullet riddled aircraft". The pilots did not want to give any respite to the Pak armour. Round the clock a cycle was maintained. It was a race against time before the Pakistani Air Force appeared on the scene, before the imponderables of war could neutralize the advantage.

Gosain now made a wide sweep over the field to take stock of the situation before joining the fray. And then he noticed it. An enterprising band of eight tanks having disengaged from the battlefield by making a wide detour was racing on the pucca road towards Jaisalmer. It was a bold attempt, but futile. What followed was sheer slaughter. No pilot could dream of a better target— tanks lined up in a row over the road, all sitting ducks, all for the taking.

In the meantime, the Army Divisional Headquarters had realized that Pakistan had made a bold gamble at Laungewala, so the Indian armour was ordered to reverse its gear and rush back to Laungewala in full throttle. By evening, the armour arrived and joined in 17 sorties were flown on the first day, i.e. 5 December 1971.

Pakistani armour had also sent an SOS for urgent reinforcement, specially air cover. An intercepted message for air cover read—"*Jaldi Madad bhejo. Yahan do hawai jahaz aate hain do jate hain*" (Send us air cover quickly. Here two planes come and two depart). Moreover, from the beginning their morale had received a blow after blow. Even before the Hunters appeared, one of our pilots-Yadav-hit a jeep with rare aim, judging from the long distance. It was apparently carrying a high-

## Narrations of a Fighter Pilot

ranking Pak officer as, soon after, the jawans saw one Pak helicopter landing behind a huge sand-dune and a body from the jeep being put in it. Then the helicopter left in a huff. PAF did not provide any air cover, SOS notwithstanding, though reinforcements were sent forthwith.

But the reinforcements did not reach the Pak armour. The Hunters were waiting. "By mid-day, I sighted," reported Jagbir after the mission, "a huge convoy of tanks, guns, armoured personnel carriers and other vehicles mounted on railway wagons accompanied by troops approaching the Khairpur railway station near Gabbar". Once again the Hunters poured rockets and cannon fire till the whole train was a burning wreck. That was the end of "Operation Laungewala", so far as Pakistan was concerned. "And that was also the end of the traditional grandiose dreams of the Pak generals based on the myth of invincibility of their armour. They had played the gamble before with relative impunity. But then a gamble is a gamble," he narrates.

In this battle the normal demand and implementation procedures for Close Air Support were discarded. When an aircraft was ready it was launched. The Pakistani army must have got their Air Force to react at last. During the night, at about 4.45 a.m., the approaching drone of piston engines was heard. The anti-air craft guns opened up, forcing the PAF C-130 Hercules to turn back, dropping its 31 bombs just outside the Jaisalmer airfield perimeter fence. An underground power cable and a telephone pole were hit leading to loss of power and communications for a while.'

Relentless air action against the enemy continued on 6 December. The tanks had dug-in, which made spotting and attack accuracy a little difficult. During the battle it was reported that enemy was seen abandoning their tanks and other vehicles and running away. Their fighting potential was in ruins and their morale was even worse. Eighteen sorties were flown. By the time the battle ended, the Pakistanis had lost 37 of about 59 tanks along with numerous other tracked and wheeled vehicles which were destroyed or damaged.

Major Atma Singh, the AOP, too had his share of luck. His aircraft's engine failed while flying in the battle area. He landed his light observation aircraft 'Krishak' on the Helipad at Laungewala. As he jumped out he saw a Pakistani jeep with a bazooka bearing down on his aircraft. He quickly leapt into the aircraft, put on his radio and directed one of the Hunters to strafe the jeep. The AOP aircraft, though hit, was saved by the brave Major Atma Singh. Later it was brought to Jaisalmer airfield by an IAF Pilot. It was an episode straight from the movies.

It was only with the timely help of the Air Force that Laungewala was saved. The first few sorties were flown by Flight Lieutenant Gosain, Flight Lieutenant D.K. Das, Squadron Leader R.N. Bali and Flight Lieutenant Deepak Yadav under the command of Wing Commander Minhi Bawa. The pilot officers participating in the war also included Deepak Datta, brother of film director J.P. Datta (who later made the blockbuster movie titled 'Border'.) Deepak was handling ATC communications at the Jaisalmer air base.

According to Minhi Bawa, the most significant contribution of the IAF during the battle was that it threatened the Pakistani force and frustrated it. "We intercepted a Pakistani message, saying that the "enemy Air Force is giving us a tough time. It is impossible to advance. Please send air force for cover immediately or retreat will be impossible". The enemy Air Force was not up due to some inexplicable reasons. Our own aircraft kept on coming and pinning down the enemy. They came in waves of two and four. They were extremely skilful and daring; not even a single rocket missed the target. The moment a rocket would hit a tank it would burst into flames like a bonfire."

The achievement of the IAF was best summed up by the GOC of 12 Div, Major General R.F. Khambatta who has gone on record to say—"Nowhere in the recent 14 days war have so few achieved so much, with such little loss at Laungewala". How very correct was he! "We flew a total of 222 sorties during the Laungewala Battle" says Minhi Bawa.

For the IAF, this battle will be written in the golden letters and will go down in the annals of history as one of the most historic battles and an event of great significance, whereas for Pakistan it was the darkest hour. To commemorate the gallant action taken by a limited number of Indian Air Force personnel to defend their motherland against almost impossible odds, a three sided Victory Pillar had been erected at Jaisalmer, rather than anywhere else, because it was from here that the battle was fought and won. This was unveiled by the then Defence Minister Shri Jagjivan Ram on 9 Dec 1977.

Whenever the topic of Laungewala comes up the question always arises as to how come we were successful against such staggering odds? The answer is simple. The will and determination to hold on at all costs by Kuldip and his men and the lack of drive and determination on the part of the Pakistani Commander.

Not only were they pushed back across the border but our forces also advanced into Pakistan. They left behind on the battlefield 37 tanks, nearly 200 vehicles and over 100 dead. The body of an army dog was also found on the battlefield presumably brought by them to locate mines. The Pakistanis had to retreat in defeat and humiliation. Their divisional and brigade commanders both were sacked after this action.

For this battle the IAF and AOP personnel jointly earned 22 honours and awards. Wing Commander Minhi Bawa was awarded the AVSM, while Vir Chakras were awarded to Squadron Leaders R.N. Bali, F.J. Mehta, Jagbir Singh, D.K. Das, Flight Lieutenants K.S. Suresh, Romesh Gosain, M.P. Premi. Amongst the AOP officers, Major Atma Singh and Captain PPS Sangha also received Vir Chakras. The other awardees were recipients of Sena Medals and Mentioned-in-Despatches.

# 10

## The War in other Fronts—
## A Resume

While the battle of Laungewala was just one amongst scores of others fought in both the eastern and western fronts, it will be prudent to take stock of the overall developments in both the fronts, briefly and chronologically, with a view to give the readers an overview.

The declaration of war by both India and Pakistan has already been covered in an earlier chapter. On 5 December, in concert with the Mukti Bahini, Indian forces liberated some territory in Bangladesh. A Pakistani brigade sized attack near Poonch in J&K, with the main thrust coming from Kahuta near the Haji Pir Pass, was also beaten back. Coming to the seas, a task force of the Indian Navy, in a bold attack on Karachi harbour the previous night, sent to the bottom two Pakistani destroyers, namely, PNS 'Khaiber' and 'Shahjehan'.

Karachi harbour installations were also pounded. In another operation in the Bay of Bengal, the Indian Navy sank an enemy submarine PNS 'Gazi' and launched round the clock bombardment of the ports of Chittagong and Cox's Bazar. Indian Naval planes also pounded military targets and installations in Khulna, Chalna and Mangla ports, Chittagong airfield and numerous other military targets nearby.

Approximately two brigades of Pakistani troops, supported by an armoured regiment, launched an attack on Indian positions in the Chhamb sector of J&K. In the UN Security Council that day the Soviet Union vetoed an American resolution calling for immediate end to hostilities and withdrawal of forces from each other's territory.

The next day Indian forces evacuated Chhamb in J&K in the face of relentless enemy pressure, but not without knocking out 23 T-59 Pakistani tanks.

In the eastern sector Indian forces captured Feni and Hilli posts. Other gains included Nawabganj, 32 km south of Rangpur, and Jaintiapur in the north-eastern corner of Sylhet district. Sultanpur, on the route from Akhaura to Brahmanbaria, was also captured. The Indian Prime Minister announced in Parliament India's recognition of Bangladesh, following which Pakistan broke off diplomatic relations with India.

On 7 December, Jessore in Bangladesh was liberated by Indian forces. In the same sector, the vital communication centre of Jhenida fell while the capture of Meherpur opened the way to Chuadanga and Kushtia. The smaller towns of Sarsa and Mancharpur were

## The War in other Fronts—A Resume

liberated. Lalmonirhat airfield was also captured by Indian forces. In another sector Indian troops, after landing in helicopters freed Sylhet and Maulvi Bazar from Pakistan Army's control.

In Jammu & Kashmir an area east of Chhamb known as 'Chicken's Neck' was occupied by Indian forces. This affected the capture of 71 sq km of enemy territory. That apart, an Indian thrust towards Sialkot cut 19 km deep into Pakistani territory. In Rajasthan, Indian troops made deep inroads in the Barmer sector. In Kutch, the posts of Jaleli, Kalebaig and Chhad Bet were captured by Indian troops. The United States of America and other countries took the issue to the General Assembly under the 'Uniting for Peace' resolution. The Assembly called for immediate ceasefire and withdrawal of troops.

On 8 December Comilla and Brahmanbaria in the east were also captured, placing the entire sector opposite Tripura under Indian control. Indian forces advanced towards the river ports of Chandpur and Daudkandi, liberating Elliotganj.

On the western front, Indian troops captured an area of 2,070 sq km in the Barmer sector. Further south, in Kutch, a commando raid towards Virawah was launched. Further up in the north-west, Indian forces captured Takhtpur, 16 km north-east of Dera Baba Nanak. Two posts near Kargil were also taken. On 9 December Indian Navy went into action off Karachi again, destroying three more Pakistani warships, doubling the enemy's losses. The sinking of the submarine PNS 'Ghazi' on the night of December 3/4 was formally announced by Pakistan.

In the east, three river ports of Chandpur, Daudkandi and Ashuganj were occupied. Jamalpur in Sylhet district was surrounded by Indian troops. First signs of a Pakistani crack-up was discerned when Major General Rao Farman Ali sent a message to the U.N. suing for peace. Islamabad countermanded the message.

In the west, Nagarparkar in Sind was captured. In Kashmir, nine Pakistani posts in the Kargil sector were taken. On 10 December Indian forces crossed the Meghna river and were in a position to launch an assault on Dacca. In the west Indian forces again fell back in the Chhamb sector where a Pakistani divisional sized force established a 2000 square metre bridgehead across the Munnawar Tawi river. In Kutch, Vingor and Virawah fell to Indian forces. On 11 December Indian forces captured a string of important towns such as Jamalpur, Mymensingh, Chandpur and Hilli in Bangladesh. In the west, Indian forces counter-attacked in the Chhamb sector, crossed the Munnawar Tawi river with strong IAF support and held its western bank. Pakistani losses in planes and tanks now stood at 77 and 141 respectively.

The war of liberation in Bangladesh moved to a climax on 12 December when the battle for Dacca was about to begin. Indian paratroops landed at Tangail, north of Dacca. In the west, at the northern and southern extremes of J&K, the Kargil sector was virtually swept clean of Pakistani troops while in Chhamb a determined enemy thrust was repulsed.

More enemy gunboats were sunk in the Bay of Bengal. Pakistan's naval losses now stood at 16 gunboats, three warships and two submarines, while India had lost the

## The War in other Fronts—A Resume

frigate INS 'Khukri' in the Arabian Sea earlier. On 13 December, with all eyes turned towards Dacca, there was a virtual lull on other fronts. India's largest gains were in enemy tanks, 14 of which were knocked out within the previous 24 hours, while one more was taken intact.

The nuclear-powered American aircraft carrier 'USS Enterprise', forming part of the Seventh Fleet task force of several ships and destroyers left Vietnam waters and headed for the Bay of Bengal. On 14 December Indian forces contacted Pakistani defences in Dacca for the first time. Two Indian pincers took Tangail, Joydevpur and Tungi before closing in on the Bangladesh capital. A third prong from Narsingdi advanced to within 9 km of Dacca. Chittagong harbour, pounded by Indian naval ships, was set ablaze.

Meanwhile, the civilian Governor of East Pakistan, Dr. A.M. Malik, quit his post and took refuge alongwith his family in Hotel Intercontinental which had been declared a neutral zone by the International Red Cross. Top officials of Islamabad's regime in Bangladesh resigned en masse and followed suit.

In the west, Indian thrust in the Shakargarh region results in the seizure of 900 sq km of Pakistani territory. In Sind, Indian forces gained control of the area south of the railway track in the battle of Naya Chor. The Soviet Union scuttled yet another American move in the Security Council seeking to call upon India to accept an immediate ceasefire and withdrawal of its forces from 'Pakistani territory'.

On 15 December Indian infantry columns entered Dacca. Meanwhile the US Seventh Fleet's task force headed towards the coast of Bangladesh. Japanese sources reported from Tokyo that a Soviet missile frigate and a battleship passed through Tsushima Strait and were presumably heading towards the Indian Ocean. Lieutenant General A.A.K. Niazi, commander of the Pakistani forces in Bangladesh, offered a ceasefire but General Sam Manekshaw, Chief of Army Staff of the Indian Army demanded complete and unconditional surrender by 9 a.m. the following day.

On 16 December Lieutenant General Niazi surrendered unconditionally, and India declared a unilateral ceasefire on the western front. An instrument of surrender was signed in Dacca by Lieutenant General Niazi and Lieutenant General Jagjit Singh Aurora, allied Army commander in the east. Pakistani thrust in the Pathankot-Samba sector, backed up by armour, made no headway. On 17 December Pakistan accepted India's ceasefire offer and fighting on the western front also stopped.

The Defence Minister, Mr Jagjivan Ram, gave this final tally of the 14 days war in the course of a statement in Parliament on December 18–"Indian troops alongwith the Mukti Bahini liberated Bangladesh inhabited by 75 million people. On the western front our troops occupied nearly 50 posts in the Kargil, Gurais and Uri sectors. In the Tithwal area a substantial part of the Lippa valley came into our hands. Some commanding heights were taken in the Poonch-Rajouri-Naushera sector.

The whole of the Chicken's Neck salient near Akhnur and a large area in the Shakargarh-Zafarwal salient were

## The War in other Fronts—A Resume

wrested from the enemy. The Pakistani enclave at Dera Baba Nanak was taken. Several posts were also captured on the border stretching from Dera Baba Nanak to Fazilka. In the Bikaner sector Rukanpur, Ranhal and Bijnot were captured. In the adjacent Jaisalmer sector our troops were between 6 and 12 km inside Pakistani territory. The big thrust in the Barmer area gave us effective control right up to Umarkot and Naya Chor, 45 km inside Sind.

In Kutch, a number of posts including Chad Bet were taken, and the entire Nagarparkar bulge was in our hands. Against this impressive list of gains, Pakistan could seize only a small area in Chhamb, an enclave near Hussainwala, and a lodgement in the Fazilka area. Pakistan lost 94 aircraft, 246 tanks, two destroyers, two submarines, two minesweepers and 16 gunboats. Indian losses totalled 45 planes, 73 tanks and one frigate. Nearly 93,000 Pakistani prisoners were taken captive in Bangladesh.

India lost 1,047 soldiers as dead, 3,047 as wounded and 89 as missing in Bangladesh. On the western front our losses amounted to 1,426 killed, 3,611 wounded and 2,149 missing. Pakistan has not yet announced its casualties".

Notwithstanding India's overall achievements, the battle of Laungewala stands out as a classic battle which has no parallel in the annals of military warfare.

# Bibliography

Parval, K.C., '*Indian Army After Independence*' (Lancer International, New Delhi, 1987).

Aurora, Lieutenant General J.S., Untold Inside Story – Liberation of Bangladesh' ('*Illustrated Weekly of India*', December, 1973).

Chand, N.Das, '*Hours of Glory*' (Vision Books Pvt Ltd, New Delhi, 1987).

Raghavan V.R., '*By Land and Sea*'-Punjab Regimental Centre, Ramgarh Cantt, 1987.

Bhargava, G.S., '*Their Finest Hour*'- (Vikas Publishing House Pvt Ltd, Delhi, 1972)

Khan, Fazal Muqeem 'Pakistan's Crisis in Leadership' (National Book Foundation, Islamabad, 1973)

Brian, Cloughley 'A History of Pakistan of Pakistan Army' (Oxford University Press, Karachi, 1999)

Riza, Shaukat 'The History of Pakistan Army (1966-71) (Services Book Club, Lahore, 1990)

*The Infantry India Journal*, March 1985

Personal battle accounts of various participants of the Battle of

Laungewala, to include that of Maj. Gen. R.F. Khambatta, PVSM (Retd.), Brig. R.O. Kharbanda, AVSM (Retd.), Brig. K.S. Chandpuri, MVC, VSM (Retd.), Colonel Dharam Veer (Retd.), Air Marshal MS Bawa, PVSM, AVSM, VM (Retd.), Air Commodore Ramesh Gosain, VrC, (Retd.) amongst others.

Documents provided by 23 Punjab.

Various newspaper reports of national dailies.

Directorate General of Military Operations (MO-6).

Ministry of Defence – Directorate of Public Relations.

*'Sainik Samachar'*

Ministry of Defence  -  Historical Section.

Ministry of Defence  -  Photo Section

# Index

Ajmer 51
Ali, Rao Farman, Major General 140
Alpha Company of 23 Punjab Regiment 83
AMX tanks 65, 105
Atma Singh, Major 104, 129
Aurora, J.S., Lieutenant General 58, 142
Awami League 56
Axis forces 119

Bahawalpur 62
Balbir Singh, Major 93
Baldev Singh, Havildar 101
Bali, R.N., Squadron Leader 129
Baluchis and Pathans, 38 Baluch Regiment consisting of 102
Bangladesh, 93,000 Pakistani prisoners were taken captive in 143
Bangladesh, an independent state 56
Bangladesh, Indian troops crossed into 70
Bangladesh, officials of Islamabad's regime in 141

Barmer 65
Battle, Laungewala stands out as a classic 143
Bawa, M.S. 80, 125
Bay of Bengal 138
Bewoor, G.G., Lieutenant General 62, 92, 109
Bhagi Ram, Sepoy 79
Bhairon Singh 53
Bhakhry, K.R., Captain 93
Bikaner 50
Bishan Dass, Sepoy 79
Border Security Force (BSF) 50, 85, 66
'Border', blockbuster movie titled 134
Boundary Pillars (BP) 51
Brigadier E.N. Ramadoss 92
Brigadier R.O. Kharbanda 50, 91, 95

Candith, K.P., Lieutenant General 109
Captain K.R. Bhakhry 93
Captain Mohammed Khan Malik 93
Captain P.P.S. Sangha 104, 136
Care and Maintenance Unit (CMU) 127

Chandpuri, Kuldip Singh, Major 50, 74, 83, 96, 113
Charan Das, Sepoy 80
'Chicken's Neck' 139
Chiddi Singh, Major 93
Commanding Officer (CO), Lieutenant Colonel M.K. Hussain 49, 113

Dacca 57
Dacca, Indian Infantry columns entered 142
Dafadar Harbir Singh 105
Datta, Deepak 134
Datta, J.P., film director 134
Defence Minister Jagjivan Ram 92, 135, 142
Deshpande, Ashok, Major 89
Dera Baba Nanak 139
Dr. Zakir Hussain, former President of India 53

East Pakistan, liberation of 55, 120
East Pakistan, suppressive action in 49

Flight Lieutenant Deepak Yadav 129
Flight Lieutenant K.S. (Koki) Suresh 129
Forward line of own troops (FLOT) 90
45 Infantry Brigade 50

Gandhi, Indira 59, 120
Ganganagar 62
General Officer Commanding (GOC) 75
General SHF J. Manekshaw 59, 142
Gosain, Romesh, Squadron Leader 129

Haji Pir Pass 137
Hameed Khan, Abdul, Major General 115, 118
Havildar Baldev Singh 101
Havildar Mohinder Singh 73
Hunter aircraft 80, 114
Hunters 129
Hussain, M.K., Lieutenant Colonel 49, 113
Hyderabad (Sind), pose a threat to 111

India and Pakistan, extremely strained relations between 49
India, Pakistan broke off diplomatic relation with 138
India's recognition of Bangladesh 138
Indian Air Force 118, 125
Indian Air Observation Post (AOP)
Indian Canberras 69
Indira Gandhi 59, 120
Indian Naval planes 138
INS 'Khukri' 141
International Red Cross 141
Islamic bond 56

Jagbir Singh 130
Jagjit Singh, Sepoy 107
Jagjivan Ram 92, 135, 142
Jaisalmer 51, 100
Jammu & Kashmir 55

Karachi 70
Karachi harbour, a bold attack on 137
Kargil 139, 142
Khambatta, R.F., Major General 50, 76, 91, 109
Khan, Barkatullah 92

# Index

Khanpur 62
Kharbanda, Brigadier R.O. 50, 91, 95
Khem Karan 84
Khokrapar 116
'Krishak', light observation aircraft 134

*Laung* or cloves, origin of its name to the trade of 51
Laungewala battle 125, 222
Sorties during the 135
Laungewala Post 49, 87
Lieutenant Colonel, M.K. Hussain 49, 83
Lieutenant Dharam Vir 53, 73, 96
Lieutenant G.S. Bajwa 93
Lieutenant General A.A.K. Niazi 142
Lieutenant General G.G. Bewoor 62, 92, 109
Lieutenant General J.S. Aurora 58, 142
Lieutenant General K.P. Candith 109

**Maha Vir Chakra 84, 106**
**Major Ashok Deshpande 89**
**Major Atma Singh 104, 129**
Major Balbir Singh 93
Major Chiddi Singh 93
Major D.S. Shekhawat 93
Major General Abdul Hameed Khan 115, 118
Major General B.M. **Mustafa** 115
Major General Fazal **Muqeem** 61, 117
Major General R.F. Khambatta 50, 76, 91, 109
Major General Rao Farman Ali 140

Major General Shaukat Riza 75, 123
Major Kuldip Singh Chandpuri 50, 74, 83, 96, 113
Malik, Captain Mohammed Khan 93
Malik, Dr. A.M. 141
Manekshaw, SHFJ, General 59
'Mata Devi', Offers prayers to 51
Mathra Dass, Sepoy (later Naib Subedar) 79
Meghna river, Indian forces crossed the 140
Mirpur Khas 62
Mohinder Singh, Havildar, 73
Mujibur Rahman, Sheikh 56
'Mukti Bahini' 57, 137
'Mukti Fauj' 57
Muqeem, Fazal, Major, General 61, 117
Mustafa, B.M., Major General 115

Niazi, A.A.K., Lieutenant General 142

Operational Training Unit (OTU) 127

Pakistan Air Force 81, 14, 132
Pakistani Thar Desert 115
Parbat Ali 116
PNS 'Gazi,' an enemy submarine 138
PNS Khaiber 137
Poonch in J & K 137
Prime Minister Indira Gandhi 59, 120
Punjab Regiment of Indian Army 49

Rahimyar Khan 50, 112
Rahman, Sheikh Mujibur 56
Raina, T.N. 59
Rajasthan 50
Ramadoss, Brigadier E.N. 92
Ramgarh 50, 100
Rann of Kutch 127
RCL gun 78
Rattan Singh, Subedar 103

Sadhewala, border village of 49, 96
Sagat Singh 59
Sangha, P.P.S., Captain 104
Sena Medal 85
Sepoy (later Naib Subedar) Mathra Dass 79
Sepoy Bhagi Ram, the cook 79
Sepoy Bishan Dass 79
Sepoy Charan Das 80
Sepoy Jagjit Singh 107
17 Rajputana Rifles 82, 93, 105
Shahgarh 51
Shekhawat, D.S., Major 93
Sheikh Mujibur Rahman, Banga Bandhu or Father of Bengal 56, 91
Sherman Tanks 63
Sikh and Dogra troops, a mix of 50
Sikkim 50
Sind 50, 52
Southern Command 109
Soviet Union Vetoed an American resolution 138
Squadron Leader Jagbir Singh 130
Squadron Leader R.N. Bali 129
Squadron Leader Romesh Gosain 129
Squadron Leader S.F. Tully 129
Suresh, K.S. (Koki) Flight Lieutenant 129

T-59 tanks 63
Thapan, M.L. 59
Thar Desert 51
13 Kumaon 92
38 Baluch Regiment 77
Tully, S.F. Squadron Leader 129
12 Infantry Division 50
23 Punjab 49

U.N. Security Council 71
United States of America 139
'USS Enterprise', nuclear-powered American aircraft carrier 141

Vijayanta tanks 65
Vir Chakra 105

Waterloo of Pakistani armour 126
West Pakistan, merciless exploitation by 56
Western Command 109
Wing Commander (later Air Marshal) M.S. Bawa 80, 125
World War 11, 119

Yadav, Deepak, Flight Lieutenant 129
Yahya Khan, General 57, 117

Zakir Hussain, Former President of India 53